I0160452

Close Encounters
of the Bovine

Close Encounters of the Bovine

Recollections of a Rural Veterinarian

Written and Illustrated by
Rosalie Cooper-Chase, DVM

Foreword by
Mark Rashid

Spinning Sevens Press

Second Edition Copyright © 2024 by
Rosalie Cooper-Chase, DVM

Copyright © 2006 by Rosalie Cooper-Chase, DVM

ALL RIGHTS RESERVED. No part of this book may be re-
produced or transmitted in any form by any means, electronic
or mechanical, including photocopying and recording, or by
any information storage and retrieval system, except as may be
expressly permitted in writing from the publisher. Requests for
permission should be addressed to Spinning Sevens Press, Attn:
Rights and Permissions, P.O. Box 440 Floyd, Virginia, 24091.

ISBN 978-0-9992465-9-7
Cover design by Emily Kitching.

Contents

He prayeth well, who loveth well
Both man and bird and beast.

He prayeth best. Who loveth best
All things, both great and small;
For the dear God who loveth us,
He made and loveth all.
~Coleridge

Foreword

By Mark Rashid

I had just finished reading the manuscript of this book, *Close Encounters of the Bovine*, when I happened to mention it to a friend who has absolutely no background in livestock whatsoever.

I must say, his expression spoke volumes. It began with a slight wrinkling of his brow; then came a flaring on his nostrils, like you would do if you had just stepped in something unpleasant. After that, his expression slowly switched to one of bewilderment; as if the words "wonderful book" and "cattle" somehow didn't (nor would they ever) fit together comfortably in the same sentence. I suppose there are more than just a few folks out there who might feel the same way. To those folks, all I can say is—you're in for a pleasant surprise!

❊

I met Dr. Rosalie Cooper-Chase many years ago when she came to ride one of her horses in a clinic I was conducting in Texas. One of the first things I noticed about her then—and continue to see in her to this day—is her total and unmitigated compassion for animals of all kinds. What I have come to understand over the years, however, is that she holds a particularly soft spot in her heart for those animals she writes about so eloquently in this book…cattle.

You see, Rosalie understands the truth about cattle, a truth known mostly by devoted stockmen and women, along with dedicated veterinarians, like Dr. Rosalie.

❈

There was a time, not really all that long ago, when cattle were king out here in the West and in a few other parts of the country, as well. Back then, before urban sprawl and cell phones and automobiles and paved roads and fences, fortunes (and lives) were made, and sometimes lost, over cattle. Railroads built tracks westward, and towns and cities sprouted up because of the cattle. Huge tracts of land were eventually gobbled up by the cattle barons (usually where the best water could be found), and on those tracts grazed vast herds of cattle, many gathered in Texas and brought north to populate the plains that once held buffalo, by then nearly extinct.

The herds of cattle in the West eventually became so big that an easterner traveling through the West in the mid-1880s wrote home saying one could hardly throw a rock on the prairie without hitting a bovine of some kind.

Unfortunately (or fortunately, depending on what side of the fence one stands on), those days are long gone. And, while there are cattle operations still going strong in many places around the country, I believe it's safe to say the true heyday of the cattle business is pretty much over. One of the most regrettable things about this is that along with the disappearance of many of the country's large and small ranches and cattle operations also goes the loss of many of the men and women who carried with them the knowledge and understanding of the cattle they tended.

What Rosalie has so aptly done in this book is given us a glimpse of time and a way of life that may someday be gone from our landscape. It's a snapshot of people, places, and animals that, sadly, are quickly disappearing from our consciousness. The stories in this book are bound to have a profound effect on those who read them, regardless of whether you've spent countless miles in the saddle staring at the south end of northbound cattle or you've only encountered cows when you've seen them standing in a pasture as you drive by at sixty-five miles per hour.

✿

Undoubtedly, some of the stories you are about to read will make you smile. Some of them may cause you to shed a tear; and others may make you feel downright uncomfortable. Still, in the end what shines through all of them is not only Dr. Rosalie's compassion for her charges, her respect for the humans involved, and her ability to treat both with dignity, but also the honor and integrity with which her work is performed.

My guess is by the time you've finished reading *Close Encounters of the Bovine*, you will hope, in the same way so many others already do, that if one of your animals were in trouble, someone like Dr. Rosalie Cooper-Chase would already be in a truck heading your way.

I think sometimes we need to take a step back and just remember we have no greater right to be here than any other animal.
~David Attenborough

Preface

This book is a slightly updated version of the original book titled *Close Encounters of the Bovine*. I was encouraged to re-publish the book after the first publisher went out of business. Tom Moates of Floyd, Virginia, Equestrian Journalist and Author as well as owner of Spinning Sevens Press, was the person who took on the task of having these stories go into a second edition. I will be forever grateful for his help and encouragement.

I graduated from Texas A&M University College of Veterinary Medicine in 1986. I bought the South Pine Animal Hospital, located in the small town of Crockett in Houston County, Texas, in 1987 and was a practicing veterinarian there for twenty-three plus years. I initially worked as a mixed animal practitioner; that is, I worked with just about any animal that needed help. Mostly dogs and cats, though I found the large animal part of my work with cattle, horses, plus a few sheep, goats and pigs, especially rewarding in so many ways. I loved my job. I sold my practice to a young veterinarian in 2010, going in on occasion when asked by the new owner to come help out with a case. I retired from veterinary work in 2019.

Horses were why I got into veterinary medicine—horses and cats. I love cats. My love of those two species was the main reason I sweated through years of pre-veterinary studies, why I struggled through four years of veterinary college, and why I wanted to be employed only in a mixed practice once I graduated.

Ah, but cows. Why a book about cows? Why did I want to work with cows to begin with? I didn't grow up around cows.

Our family didn't have cows; the milk we drank as children usually came in a powered form. I didn't know much about cows in general until I was a teenager living in North Carolina. I worked at a horse farm, assisting the elderly gentleman owner with his animals, including milking a few dairy cows he kept. He unfortunately had suffered a stroke that greatly affected his ability to work with his cows and horses, yet he never missed a day to go out to the farm where he kept his animals. I spent almost all my spare time out at that farm, working and learning all I could. I learned a lot from that man. He taught me much about animals over the years I helped him on his farm. I'll never forget him.

I really learned about cows, grew to like them, appreciate them, and wanted to work with them when I was in my 20s, employed as a veterinary assistant at a clinic in Rosenberg, Texas.

Regular people don't often get up close and personal with cows, certainly not as they do with puppies or kittens. Due to the lack of much human interaction with cattle, cows often get a bum rap in public relations. The average person does not seem to think of cows as being very smart. They appear only to stand around a lot, eating grass. Cows are thought to be good for mainly just three things—milk, meat, and leather. Yet cows are very good at being what they are. No other animal on earth is as good at being bovine as a cow is. For what they were designed to be and do, cows are the best.

One of the things that drew me into veterinary medicine was my empathy for animals, all animals. During my veterinary career, it was my desire to do the best thing possible for any animal I was presented with by anyone, owner or not. It was often not an easy job, and not all the owners of a pet left with me to treat, cared as much for their pet's comfort and well-being as

I thought they should. I viewed animals not as lesser beings but as creatures no less deserving of compassion and good care than are the members of the human species.

My own opinion about animals and the world in general was and is that animals and the world were created, yes for our use, but firstly to please God the Creator. And I'm sure that animals do just that and do it very well. Animals go about their business honestly, being the best at what they were created to be.

Animals would seem to have no desires other than to be comfortable and well fed, with the kindness and friendship of fellow creatures as a bonus, be it of the same species or of another that chooses their companionship. Animals do not aspire to wealth; a cardboard box with an old towel thrown in is just as satisfying to a purebred Persian cat as it is to a homeless old alley cat. Dogs are perfectly content to hang out with their packs, canine or human, with no regard to whether the house is a mansion in town or a shack in the woods. A horse would rather have the company of his mates in a field open to the extremes of the weather than the loneliness of the most luxurious stall. And a cow would never barter her milk and offspring for feed and a clean stall. She only asks to be treated fairly and with dignity. And what's wrong with that?

These few stories are little slices of my life as a large-animal practitioner in East Texas. Most of my clients who owned cattle had only a few head, and they liked their cows, not only as a source of income but as fellow travelers on this planet. I appreciated those people most who considered their animals' well-being first, who didn't think about how much it might cost before they called on my assistance to help restore a cow's health or save a calf. I liked people with consideration for their animals, as it made my job easier and more enjoyable. To see a newborn calf lying on the ground, struggling for his first breath, to witness his first sight of the wide world around him and his first attempt to stand and nurse, to know that I saved his life and probably his mother's also—that was good stuff. Diagnosing and successfully treating a sick, suffering animal and knowing that I had a hand in its recovery was a totally exhilarating and humbling experience. I loved my job.

And so, to all those people who love their animals, who treat them with kindness and respect, thank you. To all those animals who forgive our clumsiness in our attempts to help them, thank you. And as we travel this good earth together, may God be happy with us all.

CHAPTER ONE

LOADING MR. MARTIN'S COW

An animal's eyes have the power to speak a great language.
~Martin Buber

I firmly believed that I was able to do my job as well as I did not only because of the excellent training I had in veterinary school and by real-world experience, but because of my deep respect and empathy for animals. What many people do not realize is that animals have an uncanny ability to read us humans; our body language, even our intentions toward them we are not even aware we display. When I worked with cattle and other animals, I tried to do so with a great deal of regard for their discomfort and fear of the situation. Combined with something that I can only describe as spiritual, working with cattle was often an amazing experience for me. Such was the case with Mr. Martin's cow.

Why some cows picked cold, wet days to usher their newborns into the world is a puzzle to me. It does seem to happen more often than not that the cows attempting to calve on cold wet days do need assistance. Maybe it is because the cold-weather borne calves just have less desire to slide out onto frozen ground than the temperate day calves. It could even be that we veterinarians are just a little more reluctant to go out in inclement weather, and that makes the bad weather deliveries seem more grueling and numerous. For whatever reasons, the nasty weather calvings seem to be stored in the memory banks with a little more detail than are their fair weather counterparts.

Mr. Martin had a small herd of cows in a pasture situated about twenty miles from town. Getting to his place entailed traveling some unimproved back roads. So, when he called one cold, blustery morning to ask assistance with a heifer in dystocia, a ten-dollar word that means "difficult birth," it was all I could do to suppress a moan. Could he possibly trailer her to the clinic? No, that was not possible. His trailer was in the shop having the floorboards replaced. He expected that I'd have to go out to see the cow.

I'll admit, it was with great reluctance that I climbed into my truck for the drive out to the Martins. Besides being in the middle of nowhere, the ranch was situated in the river bottom, smack in the middle of some of the lowest-lying land in the county. Water after a rain stayed on that ground forever. We'd recently had some torrential rains and I figured the Martin place would be ankle deep in water, mud and mire. To add to the attraction of the place, pens were non-existent. Mr. Martin depended on stout ropes and nearby trees or fence posts to restrain cattle needing work. How he managed to load cattle for a trip to the sale barn was unknown to me. Now I had a call to go out there and help a struggling cow. I sighed, pulled my coat around me just a little tighter, put the truck in gear, and began my journey to the ranch at the end of the world.

The drive out was as expected—the road up to the ranch was slick with mud and treacherous. Mr. Martin met me at the gate with his tractor and a tow chain— always a bad sign. He signaled that I should follow. I put the truck in low gear, and moved down the lane behind the tractor. We seemed to be surrounded by water, with the only high point around being the roadbed over which we slowly traveled. A fine mist of rain was falling, adding to the gloom of the day. I kept my eyes on the old man where he sat ramrod straight on the metal seat of an ancient tractor that popped and farted exhaust into the chilly air. Mr. Martin raised his hand to indicate a stop, and I let the mud sucking on the tires of my truck pull my Dodge to a stand still. Since he was climbing down from the tractor, I guessed I should join him. I opened the door and slid off the seat, dropping my rubber-booted feet into frigid muddy water three inches deep. I slogged over to where Mr. Martin stood at the front of his tractor. On the roadbed about 50 feet in front of the machine lay a cow, miserable in the cold, huge with an unborn calf, her legs stiff and neck arched as she strained to rid herself of the produce of her uterus. I slogged over to check her out.

Nothing showed beneath her tail. I waded back to my truck for OB gloves and lube, then made my way back along the roadbed to the cow. She wore no halter, but a short lariat rope encircled her neck. There was nothing nearby, no tree, no post, to secure it to. However, it was evident that the poor cow was not going to be getting up and running away any time soon. She rolled her upside eye to me, the white of her eye showing large. I checked her general condition, and cringed at her small size. Mr. Martin had told me the cow was only 16 months old. She had come into her first heat nine months earlier while still on her own mamma, turned out with a big crossbred Hereford bull. She might have weighed 500 pounds without the calf inside her. She was thin and rough-coated, but her udder was strutted, full of milk for the unborn calf. She groaned and strained fruitlessly to expel the calf from her body.

The ground was cold and muddy where I knelt behind the heifer. I shivered as the wet chill from the ground penetrated my overalls and jeans and caused me to shiver all over my body. I pulled on the shoulder length plastic OB gloves, cleaned the cow's rear end with soap and the warm water from my gallon jug, lubed up my hands, and inserted my right hand into her vagina, wondering what I could find.

Immediately, my fingers encountered two enormous hooves encased in the rubbery white covering of the calf's hooves, nature's way of protecting the uterus from injury by the calf's hooves. Just behind the hooves was the head of the calf, the size of which exceeded the diameter of the birth canal. When my fingers tested for a suckle reflex, the calf's response was immediate and strong. Very much alive, but there was no way this calf would enter the world the way God had intended. A Caesarean section was the only way both cow and calf could be saved.

I stood up, stripping off the long OB gloves as I turned to Mr. Martin, who stood silently holding the end of the cow's rope. I must have been tired or cold, or both. For a moment, my mind flashed a picture of this thin old man tethered to this cow who, only in my mind, had leaped up and was galloping frantically across the watery pasture, the rancher still hanging onto the rope, flapping like a pennant in her wake. I shook my head and jumped back into reality. Mr. Martin looked at me quizzically.

"Calf's too big to come out," I informed him. "But it's alive and pretty strong right now. If we want to save it and the cow, we'll have to do a C-section."

Mr. Martin glanced around as if searching for something, holding the rope firmly in his two knotty old hands. "I can tie her off to the tractor," he said helpfully. "That way I'll be able to help you git that calf out."

Few of these old ranchers seemed to understand what went into delivery by C-section. To do major surgery in field conditions that defied any concession to sanitation was ridiculous. I pretended to mull over his offering.

"Mr. Martin," I said, shaking my head sadly, "we're going to have to get her to the clinic. It's too wet and dirty out here to think we can do the surgery here. I know your trailer's in the shop, but can you borrow one to bring her into town?"

I watched the thought processes turn over in Mr. Martin's head. After a few moments, he nodded. "Ben Gerick lets me use his trailer sometimes," he said. "I'll have to go home to call him."

"Good." I turned to the cow. "Let's get her up and to the gate, at least. If she stays on her feet, it'll slow down the contractions a little so maybe the calf won't die before we can do the surgery."

He nodded his understanding and we coaxed the tired heifer to her chest, then to her feet. I was amazed that she was able to get up at all. She walked, spraddle-legged, down the muddy road before us as we urged her around the tractor and my truck, toward the gate. At the high ground near the gate, Mr. Martin tied the rope to one of the posts that felt the most securely seated in the wet ground. As long as she was standing up, the cow did not appear to be straining as much. That was good. Mr. Martin went back for his tractor and I for my pickup, and we both headed down the mud road to the main gate. I would prepare for the surgery in the dry cleanliness and relative warmth of my clinic's barn, and he would enlist some help and borrow a trailer to haul the suffering cow. Mr. Martin figured it would take him about an hour and a half to get to the clinic.

At the clinic, I informed my crew what was going to be happening in the next couple of hours. We rescheduled afternoon appointments and prepared for the surgery. A space heater cranked out a small measure of warmth into the chilly barn where the chutes and pens were set up and waiting for the patient. My instrument packs, gloves, and supplies were at the ready. We waited. And waited.

Two hours, Mr. Martin and the cow still hadn't appeared. I had my receptionist call the Martin house. His wife informed us she had not seen him in two hours, not since he had come in and told her he was going with his three friends, Ben Gerick, Franklin Grief, and Lawrence Brown, to get the cow with Ben's trailer. I clicked off the names in my head. I knew Ben Gerick and Franklin Grief. Both were elderly gentlemen like Mr. Martin, retired long years from their careers, spending their time tending their small herds of cows and waiting for their social security checks to come in. I didn't know Mr. Brown, but my guess was he was of the same generation. I worried about these old men, out in the cold, misting rain, standing in near freezing water while trying to load a reluctant cow into a strange trailer. Though she was small, 500 pounds of cow resisting arrest was trouble. After fretting about the situation for another hour, I decided to go out to the ranch and see what was happening.

As I approached the ranch gate I could see there were two vehicles, as well as Mr. Martin's old tractor, on the lane inside the pasture. One of the pickups had a 14-foot stock trailer hitched to it. The only relatively dry spot left to park was on the county road, so I stopped and got out of my truck and worked my way, rubber-booted, through the slick mud to the pasture.

Mr. Martin came around the vehicles to greet me. They had managed to back the trailer into the pasture so that it was as close as possible to where the cow had been left tied. Behind the trailer stood Mr. Martin's three friends. Mr. Brown was just as I suspected, another senior citizen, rubber-booted, wearing a tattered old coat and a toboggan cap pulled down over his ears against the cold and wet. All four of the elderly gents looked cold, wet and tired. The cow was still tied, but now the rope ran from her head through the trailer and out one side where Mr. Grief held the end, keeping the rope taut. The cow was squatting on her rump, front feet out and braced in front of her in the muddy ground. She wanted no part of the trailer.

Around her on the ground lay some logging chains, probably 20 feet in length each. A broken rope dangled from the trailer. I could feel the hair on the nape of my neck rise, even under my wool cap. This had been going on for three hours? This poor cow had been struggling against these ropes and chains and determined old men for three hours? I wondered how in the world her calf could still be alive through that. I wondered how this underweight, pregnant cow could still be resisting her capture after three long hours. As I stood numb, taking in the story the scene told me, Mr. Martin spoke up.

"We tried pulling her with the tractor, but the rope broke," he informed me, indicating the frazzled end of a rope dangling from the trailer. "We tried making a come-along around her butt with the chain, but that didn't work none either. We tried a hot shot, but all that did was make her mad." He paused to let that information sink into my mind. "We was fixing to try pushing her in with the tractor next," he finished.

Mr. Brown, a tall, pot-bellied, balding man well into his 80s, coughed from his position on the other side of the trailer. "What we need," he said loudly, hooking his thumbs into his sagging pants' belt loops and hitching them upward, "What we need is a couple more men to help us get her in."

"That's it!" agreed Mr. Grief immediately. "With two more men, we can pick this cow up and set her right in the trailer!"

My mind quickly generated a motion picture of six old geezers in ragged winter gear hoisting up this wet, tired cow, three on each side, and racing with her into the trailer. Six old men yelling "Huthuthut!" in unison as they bore the wretched beast rapidly along. I must have been getting a little too cold and tired, too. Again, I shook my head to clear this new mental image.

I had moved to stand beside the trailer to keep watch on the cow, positioned so I also could look into the trailer. I tried to see what looked so terrifying to the cow that she preferred arguing against ropes and chains and old men, rather than mount up into the only dry area around. Nothing was in the trailer. I looked down at the cow. She was squatting down hard against the rope, a fine, white foam forming around her muzzle, her eyes bulging from the effort of resistance. As I looked pityingly down at her, she rolled her eyes up to meet mine.

"Yep, two more men, and maybe some more chain," intoned one of the old men.

I shook my head in sorrow for the cow. I leaned

over her slightly, and whispered to her *sotto voce.* "It would be best if you just got in the trailer," I urged her. "Before they bring in re-enforcements."

The heifer's eyes went a little larger, and suddenly, she stood up, so quickly that Mr. Grief, on the other end of the lariat, stumbled backwards and lost his grip on the suddenly slack rope. The cow continued to look directly at me, and I at her. She turned her head and faced into the trailer, pitched her ears forward, took a tentative step forward and snuffled at the trailer floor for a couple of seconds. Then graciously, with all the dignity she could muster, she stepped up onto the trailer floor.

For a minute, the stunned silence of the shocked men was all that was heard besides the creaking of the trailer as the cow moved forward over the wooden floor boards. I was just as stunned as they were. Then, coming awake, I slapped my jaw shut, stepped back and swung the tailgate closed.

Mr. Martin was staring, open-mouthed, at the cow standing quietly in the trailer.

"Let's go," I suggested, acting as if the miracle that had just occurred had been totally expected; exactly what I hoped to happen. All four men suddenly jumped into action, picking up their chains, securing the trailer tailgate, running as fast as their old bones could carry them to their vehicles for the drive to town. I hustled to my own truck, did a careful U-turn on the muddy surface of the road, and led the caravan to the clinic.

It was a successful surgery. The calf, unbelievably, was still alive; vigorous and strong. The cow, her ventral abdomen sporting a row of neat sutures, stood up almost immediately after the surgery. Once released from her restraints, she lowed to her calf and washed it tip to toe. Both of them recovered fully, and left for their home ranch after 48 hours in the clinic.

※

Mr. Martin and his cronies still talk of me whispering into that heifer's ear that day, suggesting she stand up and get in the trailer. I don't know why she did what she did, and so dramatically. Maybe it was she felt my empathy and desire to help her. Maybe she was just tired of fighting. Maybe, too, the calf squirmed in the uterus and caused the cow to shift her weight enough that she could stand up, causing the rope applying the pressure to loosen and giving her a chance to make the choice of going into the trailer. I don't know, but I don't argue with the power that saved a cow and calf that day, and allowed four old men to come in out of the rain.

CHAPTER TWO

MR. MASON'S EVASIVE COW

*It is just like man's vanity and impertinence to call an animal
dumb because it is dumb to his dull perceptions.*
~Mark Twain

It happened more than once, that unexplained but
awesome experience of a cow seeming to read my mind
or feel my empathy for her situation so that she was
suddenly cooperative with my efforts to help her.

Mr. Mason was an older rancher who was not a
regular client of mine. With an apologetic tone in his
voice he made it perfectly clear he was asking for my
help only because he couldn't get hold of his regular
vet. I did a lot of emergency call-outs for that reason
for other people and had ceased being offended for

being the last choice in the phone book for an animal owner seeking veterinary assistance.

Mr. Mason was a gentleman and known locally for his kindness and consideration of others. I told him I would be happy to help him out of the crisis with his laboring cow. With directions in hand and Barbara, the high school girl working for me after classes that year in the passenger seat of the pickup I used for farm calls, I headed out to the country on that pretty, early fall day.

The cattle pens on Mr. Mason's ranch were immaculate; the fences high and strong, the head gate well greased and in perfect working order. Mr. Mason met us at the gate. The problem I saw right away was that the cow wasn't in the pens. She was down, lying out in the field. The rancher explained that he had been unable to get her to stand up. There was one small calf hoof showing from her vulva, he said, but she had not progressed in the labor in the previous two hours. She was an older cow and had calved many times before. He knew she was in trouble. He was worried about losing both her and her calf.

He led the way on his four-wheeler; Barbara and I followed him across the pasture in my work truck. I drove a Dodge pickup outfitted with a vet box carrying all the supplies and equipment I might need on a large animal call. Mr. Mason raised Red Brangus; large, deep red cattle of good size, with long ears and loose skin. The Brahman breeding in his cows was evident, and he said they were good momma cows.

Unfortunately, coyotes and feral dogs had been raiding the local herds and killing calves. In defense of his calves, Mr. Mason had acquired and now kept a male donkey with the herd of cows with calves. The donkey did a great job of guarding the calves from the marauding dogs and hungry coyotes. However, the donkey was leery of people and kept the cows moving away from any humans who did not match his idea of acceptable. The donkey regarded the old rancher on his four-wheeler kindly. My red pickup was another story. It put up a red flag in the donkey's mind, and he turned to his charges and hustled his adopted herd away into the trees.

Mr. Mason's property was beautiful. His large pastures were spotted with some on the tallest, straightest pine trees in Houston County. They were so tall, their lowest branches were at least 20 feet up, and the sun easily reached the grass under the trees' canopies. There was very little brush or weeds. It was easy to keep track of the cattle as the donkey herded the 25 or so cows with their calves out of harm's way of my deadly pickup. The cow Mr. Mason was concerned with was left lying in the open, down on her side, laboring to deliver a calf that wouldn't budge from her uterus. As we drove nearer the cow, we could see a white hoof of a calf showed at the vaginal opening.

Mr. Mason was able to drive his little four-wheeler right to the cow's side. As he pulled up next to her, she stopped her straining and sat up on her chest. I was disappointed to see the cow did not have a rope on her head or around her neck. I hoped she was not going to jump to her feet and leave as Mr. Mason fumbled with the lariat he had brought along with him on his four-wheeler. Cows have a way of being able to leap up and run, even with a calf wedged in their pelvic canal. I've seen them moving with surprising speed even while in the throes of heavy labor. I've even seen one leap a five-foot fence like a gazelle, a half-way born calf dangling from her. I much preferred to arrive at a ranch with the cow already penned, or at least securely tied with a rope to something stout. Evidently, Mr. Mason had assumed his cow would not be able to get up, and had not taken my advice to put a rope on her before I got there.

But it was too late. The cow had spotted my truck. She came to full alert, and stumbled to her feet.

The one foot of the calf she was trying to deliver disappeared into her depths. Mr. Mason tried to flip the rope over her head, but she easily tossed it aside, watching my truck with pronounced trepidation. She turned suddenly and took off for the rest of the herd that was quickly disappearing into the outer reaches of the pasture.

I drove over to where the rancher stood with his empty lariat. We conferred. Mr. Mason was positive he could bring the entire group of cows around the edge of the pasture and to the pens, where we could separate out the cow in trouble and deliver the calf. Mr. Mason was an elderly man, gentle and easy in his manner. His concern for the cow was great. "I don't want the cow to suffer anymore," he said. "This won't take long."

He cranked his four-wheeler and took off toward the herd. True to his plans, the cows circled the edge of the pasture and headed in the direction of the pens, the target cow somehow gamely keeping up with the herd. The donkey, however, was worried about strangers in the pasture, and made other plans for his herd. Once within sight of the pens, he commenced to drive the cows away from the suspected danger. Using teeth and hooves, his long ears flat to his head, he drove the group of cattle past the pens and back into the safety of the pasture. We could do nothing as the main group of cows headed back into the pasture, our patient doing her best to keep up with them.

We conferred again. Mr. Mason said he could get the donkey out of there, allowing us to handle the herd without its interference. He had a small bucket of grain on his four-wheeler and drove out to try to lure the donkey within his reach. While the donkey took the bait, Mr. Mason slid a rope over its head. He then tied the little donkey firmly to a tree. The cows, now without their guardian, should have been easier to herd.

They were not. For whatever reason, not one of those cows would go near the pens. Every time we got them close, one of them would spook and take off, with two, three, and finally all the rest of the cows chasing after her. We abandoned our vehicles and attempted to herd the cows on foot. We fanned out across the pasture, attempting to haze the herd toward the pens. It was no use. It appeared that one old man, a teenage girl, and a female veterinarian were no match for a group of cattle determined not to be penned. The target cow was fatiguing, and labor was forcing her to slow appreciably. Finally, she stopped and lay down while the other cows drifted away from her.

Mr. Mason again tried to approach her with the rope, but she was wise to him and his motives now. She lumbered to her feet and trotted away. I was no cowboy; throwing a lariat was not on my meager list of cowboy skills. I tried, though. There was no doubt that the cow would remain safe from me. Barbara had done a little roping with her high school rodeo club and thought she might be able to get a rope over the cow's head. The trick would be to get close enough to the cow to make throwing a loop a good option.

The cow had given up trying to keep up with her herd mates. Nonetheless, it was obvious that she was determined not to be roped. She was equally determined not to be hazed into the pens. She was walking slowly, lying down when she got some distance from us, jumping up when we got near, and then doubling back on us toward the pasture, over and over. After about the sixth attempt to pen her, Mr. Mason called me over for another conference. We'd been chasing the cow for close to two hours. Evening was falling. The cow was at this point heading away from the pens, a clear shot for the wide pasture in front of her. Our chances of catching her looked pretty hopeless. She stopped to grunt and strain against a contraction, the calf's one foot making an appearance before once again sliding out of view.

"I can't stand to see her suffer," Mr. Mason told me. "It looks like we're not going to catch her. The calf's probably dead by now anyway. I'm going to go back to the house, get my gun, and put her out of her misery.

You ladies might as well go on home."

We stood quietly watching the cow as she strained then moved further away. She was obviously in distress. I hated to see an animal suffer or die needlessly. If we could get her in the pen, I felt confident I could reposition the calf so the cow could deliver normally. However, if the owner didn't feel like we were going to catch her, I couldn't justify my time in chasing her either. Nonetheless, I felt badly for the cow as well as the owner.

"I sure hate for you to lose a good cow like that," I told Mr. Mason, shaking my head sadly. I felt my heart go out to the cow as she stumbled further away from us. Suddenly she stopped, and swung her big head towards us, both ears angled forward as if to hear every last syllable we spoke. Her big, dark eyes regarded us for a moment, nostrils flaring with her labored breath. She looked back toward the disappearing tails of the rest of the herd. After another moment, she turned and stared off toward the cattle pens behind us. With what appeared to be purposeful determination, she began to walk, then stuck out at a fast trot, circling around us.

"She's heading for the pens!" Mr. Mason exclaimed in surprise. He ran for his four-wheeler while Barbara and I scrambled for the pickup we had abandoned earlier to pursue the cow on foot. The cow disappeared between the tall trees. I was afraid she would be headed back around the edge of the field when we came out of the trees toward the pens, but No! There she was, still making a beeline for the pens!

Unbelievably, she trotted right through the gates

of the pens, Mr. Mason driving up behind her and shutting the gates. The cow trotted through the maze of pens and entered the long chute undirected by any of us. She slowed to a walk and moved down the chute all the way to the head gate. We were flabbergasted, but hurried to shut the gates and put the poles behind her, in case she changed her mind and decided she had to leave. But she showed no indication she was going to try to get away. When she reached the end of the chute, she stopped and stood panting quietly at the head gate.

We were so relieved to have caught her, and so amazed at the way in which we had, we could think of nothing to say to one another.

Rather than catching her head, we put a pole up behind her butt so she could not back up. I got my water and soap, pulled on the long, plastic OB sleeves used for the purpose, and did a quick check of the unborn calf's position. It was not a huge calf but his head and one leg were turned back into the cow and were locked behind her pelvis, preventing his birth. Because the cow had been up and moving most of the time, she had not been able to strain so much that she might wedge the calf into too tight a position. Mr. Mason had found her before she had lost too much amniotic fluid, and before the uterus had contracted tight around the calf. I had room to work in the cow.

I quickly set to righting what was wrong. I had no sooner maneuvered the calf's head and legs into the proper position when the cow gave a mighty heave, grunting with the effort. The calf practically shot out of the cow. Barbara and I caught it as it fell from the cow and eased it to the ground. He was alive. He shook his head vigorously and began to bawl in indignation. The cow answered her calf with a soft, low hum. We carried the calf out into a pen and laid him down, where he continued to snort and take in deep breaths. I did a quick check of the cow for problems, and finding none, we released the cow from the chute. She left the chute and immediately trotted over to her newborn, lowing continuously, and began to lick and clean the shiny, dark mahogany-colored bull calf.

※

It was an extremely satisfying piece of work. Mr. Mason was very grateful and happy that we were able to save both his good cow and her calf. To this day, I am in awe of the cow's sudden awareness of her fate, and her surprising decision to completely abandon her escape attempts and head for the cattle pens. She knew, somehow, with her animal intuition, that we were her only salvation.

CHAPTER THREE

COUNTRY DOGS

*Lots of people talk to animals. Not that many listen though.
That's the problem."* ~Piglet

It was an amazing thing to me that an animal could sense when a person is wanting to help it, as did Mr. Mason's cow. It was always an overwhelming feeling to receive that gift of trust from a frightened animal whose instinct was to run or fight when pain and/or confusion dictated escape. But to have that happen in reverse, to be the one needing the empathy and help, and to have an animal, or in this case, several animals, seek to help me was utterly humbling.

Cows are certainly not the only animals I've had read my mind, understand my intent, or otherwise seem to know exactly what I am up to. In my practice

I worked with cats, dogs, and horses, as well as cattle. I have a strong connection with cats, and many people brought their feline pets to me, knowing the cats would be treated with dignity and respect. Dogs that were patients or boarders in our clinic were usually calm and easy to work with, and many appeared genuinely happy to come into the building and visit with us. I found this to work out well for the animal's overall good behavior. However, the same dogs that were submissive and trusting at the clinic might behave entirely different while on their home turf, defensive of their territory and aggressive toward visitors.

Sometimes on ranch calls I had to wait for the owner to tie up or cage a dog who took offense to my presence, much like they did to mail carriers or meter readers. I understood where they were coming from, though, and rarely had a problem with the dogs after it was established in the dog's mind that the owner welcomed my visit. Subsequent calls to a ranch were usually peaceful encounters with the same dogs I'd met before. But I would not get out of my pickup on a property with a dog baying its warning at me to stay put. The night I nearly walked into a pack of guard dogs was one I won't soon forget.

It was already dark out when Mr. Lloyd called one fall day. He had penned a cow up at noon, he said, because he was sure she was going to calve at any time. Daylight Saving Time had not yet switched back to Standard Time, and when he had gotten off from his job and had gone out to check his cows earlier in the evening, it was already close to dark.

"She had the calf, Doc," he informed me. "He's OK,

but the cow prolapsed. Everything came out. I never seen one that big."

"Is she standing up?" I asked.

A prolapsed uterus was a life-threatening situation for the cow. The longer the everted uterus stayed outside the body, the higher the chance it would be damaged by trauma or impaired circulation.

"She's up," Mr. Lloyd replied. "She's nursed the calf, too. I don't want to lose her, Doc. She's a gentle thing. She's a young cow, too."

"Give me directions to your place," I said, snatching a pen off the desk, along with a note pad. He gave me directions using landmarks and mileage, as the county's roads were often poorly marked and tended to look all the same in the dark. I felt I could find the place, though, and headed for my truck.

It was a crisp, cool fall night. No moon or stars showed through the cloud cover so that the darkness was total. In the country there are no streetlights and no businesses lining the roads, casting illumination over everything. Traffic tends to be sparse after nightfall, too. I headed north out of Crockett and about ten miles out of town the white sign that read "Patterson Cemetery Road" loomed out of the dark on the side of the highway. I turned to the left off the paved highway onto the well-tended dirt county road.

It seemed that most of the back roads in Houston County were named after either a cemetery or a small country church. There were an impressive number of these cemeteries and churches in the county. Some of them dated to the 1800s. Slow to change, Houston County officials had bucked the trend going on across the state to change from named to numbered roads. Makeshift signs still pointed down various back roads with such names as "Shiloh Primitive Baptist Church Road," and "Everett Cemetery Road." The roads kept their traditional names, even when the churches had fallen down and disappeared and the cemeteries were so overgrown with grass and weeds as to cause tombstones to be invisible. I had been down Patterson Cemetery Road before, and had never seen the cemetery.

Without the added lights of other vehicles, homes, and stores, as well as there being no moon or stars in the sky, the blackness of the night was complete, except for the twin beams cast by my truck's headlights directly down the narrow road in front of me. It would be very hard to find the turnoffs ahead.

The directions said I should drive four miles after turning onto Patterson Cemetery Road, and look for a fork in the road, where a smaller road would branch to the left. I was to take that left fork. About a quarter of a mile down that road, I would be looking for a set of board fence pens just inside a pasture. Mr. Lloyd would be waiting in his pickup at the gate to the property.

After three miles, I slowed my speed somewhat, to lessen the chance of my missing the turn off. After four miles, I still had not seen a fork in the road. I crawled along, searching the dark for some break in the brushy growth along the road that might indicate a road was there. Another half mile and a dirt road branched off to the left, while the main road on which I traveled curved off to the right. It was not exactly a fork in the road but more like a lane coming in from the left. I kept on the main road a couple hundred yards more, and passed a house with lights blazing, a couple of pickups and cars in the yard.

I drove slowly for another half of a mile. By now I was five miles from the highway, a mile past where Mr. Lloyd said the fork onto an unmarked road would be. Frustrated, I made a U-turn in the road, and retraced the road to the house and the lane that had appeared to fork off to the left as I had approached the house earlier. I made a right turn onto that dirt lane.

The house's lights disappeared behind me as I drove along the narrow lane. The lane was very narrow and the roadside weeds and brush were so close to my truck I could reach out the window and touch them. This sure didn't look like the right road. I decided to find a place to turn around, and go back toward the highway, feeling I'd missed the proper turn after all.

The lane did not widen and no side roads appeared out of the gloom. The lane was taking a decidedly steep downward pitch. The roadbed appeared to be turning to sand, and my truck struggled to move along the slippery surface.

I must have traveled at least a quarter mile when ahead of me in the dark loomed a closed and apparently locked shiny aluminum gate, 16 feet wide. The weeds encroached upon the road right up to the gateposts. Great. No way to turn around. I'd have to back out.

I put the truck in reverse and eased my foot onto the accelerator as I looked over my right shoulder out the rear window. Unfortunately, my truck did not have 4-wheel drive. The truck's tires caught, then slipped, and started spinning in the sand. The incline of the road was so steep and the sand so slippery and loose, if I continued to press the accelerator, I would cause the tires to dig great troughs and bury the axle. Shoot, I muttered, or words to that effect.

I put the truck in neutral, found my flashlight and got out. I aimed the light onto the left rear tire. Not quite to the axle, but getting there. I turned the beam to the gate, hoping that it was unlocked so I could drive into the pasture and make a U-turn and drive out onto the lane again. I inspected the latch end of the gate. A chain with a padlock encircled it and the post. The padlock was secured. I kicked the ground in frustration. My truck rumbled in sympathy.

I did not have a car phone or a two-way radio with which to call for help. I got back into the cab, put the truck in reverse, and tried to back out again. This time the tires spun madly, flinging sand out from beneath them, and settling the truck deeper into the sand. I cut off the engine, got out, and turned my flash light beam under the truck to inspect the rear axle. What axle? It was buried, the truck settled into the sand up to the rear bumper.

Frustrated, I squawked an unkind word at the world. It echoed in the stillness of the night. I turned off the flashlight. Man, it was dark. I quickly snapped the light on again.

I would have to walk back up the lane to the house I had passed by before turning down this lane. Mr. Lloyd had given me a cellular phone number to call, if I did get lost on my trip to his place. I did not have a cell phone. I was lost, alright. Perhaps I could use the phone at that house to call Mr. Lloyd and let him know where I was and why I was delayed. I locked the truck, buttoned my coat and, flashlight in hand, started up the steep, sandy lane.

It was a bit steeper than I had realized. Shining the flashlight back toward my pickup, all I could see was the tailgate and taillight reflections. I trudged on.

The lights of the house came into view as I topped the hill and the lane leveled out. I was about 50 yards from the house. I counted two pickups and a car in the yard. That seemed like a lot of vehicles; maybe they were having a party. I didn't intend to do more than ask for the use of their phone. Hopefully, it wouldn't be a problem.

As I stepped into the yard, still about 100 feet from the house, a dog barked, one quick, cautious canine "Who goes there?" A big dog, too, from the sound of it. I stopped in my tracks, a slight feeling of anxiety coming over me. Here I was, trespassing on some dog's territory in the middle of the night, with nothing but a flashlight to defend myself. I waited to see what the dog would do. I moved my flashlight beam, to let the animal know where I was. Silhouetted against the porch lights of the house appeared an outline of a dog. It was facing me, at full alert. It had the outline of a Rottweiler. A big, beefy dog, its massive head held high and a short tail erect and stiff. Oh great. The evening just kept getting better and better.

"Hello!" I called, hoping I sounded friendly to the dog, hoping the dog had alerted someone inside the house, who would come out to investigate if the dog barked again, maybe save my life.

The sound of my voice caused the dog to erupt into a frenzy of deep-throated baying barks, which in turn apparently alerted an entire pack of dogs, which joined the first dog in a frenzy of defensive, warning, foaming-at-the-mouth barking.

I stepped back. There was no way I would be able to outrun a pack of dogs, even if I had been wearing track shoes instead of the knee-high rubber boots I did have on. In front of me the silhouettes of a dozen dogs suddenly loomed up against the house lights, a dozen huge dogs with cropped tails and huge heads. Frightened, I backed up another step. This maneuver only served to encourage the dogs to jump toward me, baying, bellowing at the top of their lungs.

There was nothing I could do. When I did not move, the dogs held their ground and continued to fill the night air with their deafening roars. If I backed up, they advanced on me. It was safer for me to stay put and wait, hoping the residents of the house would quickly respond to their guard dogs' howls and come check on what was disturbing them.

No one came to the door of the house. The dogs continued to keep me in one place, all of them in a line at the edge of the light thrown from the porch. They did not step into the shadows where I stood, but they did not cease their barking and braying.

What was the matter with those people? Were they deaf? I couldn't hear anything coming from the house such as music or a loud television to account for their inability to notice the dogs' barking. I could certainly hear the dogs and I was sure anyone in the house could hear them also. I was positive the entire county could hear the dogs.

I couldn't shift a foot without the middle dog getting excited and lunging forward, his barks exploding louder and more threatening. If I froze in place, he would stop his advance, slow down his barking.

I realized after a moment that the dog in the middle was the biggest dog, and most probably a Rottweiler. However, the dogs that ranged out to his side were smaller. Maybe not a dozen, but there were still at least six of them, all raising Cain and facing me head on, their tails straight up over their backs. One had to be a Dachshund, yapping so enthusiastically that each soprano vocalization caused his short front legs to pop off the ground. One dog appeared to have the build of a Border Collie, and he would change positions, slink from one end of the line of dogs to the other, issue a rapid-fire bark at me, and turn and pace back to the other end to repeat the warning. A short, thick dog next to the middle and biggest dog had the outline of a bulldog, and I was sure it was his deep, gruff, intermittent bark that acted as the bass in this canine concerto. A couple of the other dogs registered as generic brands, maybe a little hound in them from the tone of their barks. All of them barked continuously and furiously. No one in the house was responding to the barrage of barking. I didn't know what to do.

Now I was getting a little annoyed, not being able to move, with no one coming to the door of the house to check on the racket the dogs were making. Unable to move an inch and frustrated with the feeling of helplessness and without meaning to, I whined out loud. The effect of my voice on the dogs was immediate and startling. They hushed as one. Absolute quiet descended again on the night air. Surprised at the dogs' response, I waited, watching their silhouettes before cautiously I tried another keening whimper. The dogs were motionless, each head cocked to one side, registering my plea.

"I'm lost and cold and tired," I whined piteously. "I have to get to Mr. Lloyd's cow and help her. My truck is stuck on the road in the sand." Every dog's head shifted abruptly, cocking in the opposite direction. They were listening. I felt encouraged. "I need help," I wheedled sadly, slumping my shoulders in despair.

The dogs were nothing but silent silhouettes against the bright house lights. I could see what they were doing, though. Stiff at attention, heads cocked at me, they started to wag their tails in short, "we hear you" movements. Even the Rottweiler's tail, though short, jerked back and forth in response to my plea. I whined again, no words, just a high-pitched, frustrated moan.

The Rottweiler ducked his head, twisted his whole body downward to the ground and, wiggling all over, came toward me. I didn't move. He slithered up beside me and grinned up at me. The other dogs then approached also, surrounding the Rott and me, all of them mimicking his posture. I was being accepted as okay, it appeared. It seemed as if they were inviting me to come on up to the house. Encouraged, I started slowly across the lawn, the half dozen dogs fawning around, licking my hand, and ingratiating themselves to me. I was emboldened. I increased my speed and strode up to the house, murmuring thanks to the dogs, patting the heads that bumped my hand, smiling at the dogs that escorted me to the porch and to the back door.

At the door, all the dogs sat down, calmly watching me, waiting for me to do whatever I needed to do next.

I peered through the glass window of the storm door, on through the glass panel in the wood entrance door beyond. I could see children's school knapsacks lined up against one wall of the hallway beyond the door, but no person was within sight.

I rapped on the glass of the storm door. Before my knuckle tapped the glass a second time, a frenzied high-pitched yipping erupted from inside the house. Another dog, a small one, leapt into view through the glass. It was a Yorkshire Terrier, and it would leap wildly up to look through the window in the door, yipping shrilly, before falling out of view again. I glanced at the dogs surrounding me. Each and every one of them was grinning happily, tongues out, ignoring the yipping of the Yorkshire. Their demeanor told me it was all right to try knocking on the door again. I rapped on the glass three or four times.

All my knocking seemed to do was inspire the Yorkshire to higher leaps and sharper yips. If there was a person inside the house, they did not respond to the dog's noise or the tapping on the glass.

I looked down at the Rottweiler. He was staring intently at the doorknob. "Should I open the door?" I asked him. He opened his huge mouth and laughed up at me silently.

I tried the storm door. It was unlocked. It opened outward, and I swung it open. The Yorkshire went ballistic as I tapped on the glass panel in the wooden door. I called out a loud, "Hello!" Strangely, no one answered.

This was very weird. I looked around in the yard. With as many vehicles in the yard, why wasn't anyone answering the door? The dogs waited expectantly. I tested the doorknob. It was unlocked. I pushed the door open.

The Yorkshire went into a panic, yipping so rapidly I wondered how he could draw breath. He turned and scurried down the hall as fast as his short legs could carry him. I stepped into the entrance hall, and yodeled a "hello!" Nothing. No one answered.

I was getting very nervous about the whole situation. I took a couple steps into the house, closing the door carefully behind me. The little dog suddenly lost his nerve and fled away from me into a room to the right. He never stopped yipping, though.

I looked down at my boots, covered in sand and mud, and slipped out of them, not wishing to leave tracks on the clean tile floor. The room up ahead and to the left was brightly lit. I called out again as I eased toward the room. Still no one answered.

I sneaked a peek around the end of the wall, through the opening to the left of the entrance hall. It was a kitchen/dining room. A table was in front of me, and beyond that a service bar separated the dining area from the kitchen. The table was set with dinnerware, flat-ware, and drink glasses; place settings for ten people in total. A large basket of garlic bread, half empty, sat in the middle of the table. Spaghetti and meatballs had been served to each plate, and half of the food had been eaten before the diners had apparently dropped their forks and left the table. This was very odd. I called out again; there was no answer. The only sound was the frantic yipping of the little terrier from a room on the other side of the house.

There was a tabletop phone at the end of the counter in the kitchen. I tiptoed across the room in my stocking feet. Now I could see the entire kitchen. A big pot sat on the stove, a big bowl half filled with salad and a plate of chocolate chip cookies were on the far end of the counter. The cookies looked good. I considered trying one, but decided it was best not to tamper with the evidence.

I picked up the receiver of the phone and listened for a dial tone. Phew; there was one. I pulled the piece of paper with Mr. Lloyd's car phone number on it from my pocket, and quickly pushed in the numbers.

Mr. Lloyd answered before the phone had rung twice. "Hello?" he said, a little anxiety in his voice.

"Mr. Lloyd, this is Dr. Cooper-Chase," I said. "I'm lost. I got my truck stuck in the sand on a little road that dead-ends at a locked pasture gate. I'm using the phone in a house, but no one is here, so I don't know who lives here. I guess I missed the fork in the road I was supposed to take."

I knew I was talking rapidly, nervously. I glanced around the unnaturally quiet room. Even the little house dog had quit yipping.

"You're in a house?" Mr. Lloyd asked. "There's no house where you're supposed to be."

"I know that," I replied, feeling just a little bit exasperated. "I think I passed the place I was supposed to turn. It's pretty dark out there. I'm about four and a half miles down Patterson Cemetery Road. This house is brick with white trim. They have about six or seven dogs here. It looks like they might have a couple of kids, too, but there's no people here right now, just the dogs. The house wasn't locked, so I just came on in to use the phone. I didn't see any fence around the house. There are some pickups and a car in the yard. There's a dirt lane that goes off to the left about 50 yards before you get to the house. That's the lane I got the truck stuck on."

Mr. Lloyd was silent. "Mr. Lloyd?" I queried, wondering if I'd lost the connection.

"Wait!" he said suddenly. "I know where you are! I'll be there in about ten minutes!" He hung up before I could say another word, before I could give him the number of the phone I was using, before I could look around the kitchen for something with the family's name on it. I hung up the phone. Well, if he didn't show up in ten minutes, I'd call him again.

I really did wonder where the family was who lived in the house, who had obviously jumped up from their dinner and left, who had run off leaving the house unlocked and an assortment of vehicles parked in the yard. What was going on?

I left the dining area and went back to the entrance hall. The Yorkshire had crept out of the room he had taken refuge in, and when I emerged from the dining room he erupted into a yipping fit again, and dodged back the way he had come. I followed him into the next room, which frightened him and caused him to dart past me and retreat further into the house.

The living room had a nice lived-in look, but was

empty of any thing human. I followed the sound of the little dog's yips across the room into a narrow hallway. Doors opened on either side, presumably into bedrooms. Dare I look? What would I see if I looked? I was scared to look and scared not to look. I eased into the hallway and peeked into the first door.

The Yorkshire had hidden under the bed in that room, and he dodged under the bed skirt as I peered around the door. There was no person in there. A quick glance through the other doors revealed a bathroom, another small bedroom and across the hall from that was the master bedroom. All the rooms were devoid of people. I hurried back to the entrance hall, pulled on my boots, and eased open the door to the outside.

All the dogs were on the porch, waiting for me to reappear. They seemed genuinely happy to see me again, greeting me with licking and joyful bouncing around. They escorted me to the edge of the yard as I walked out to the lane to wait for Mr. Lloyd, but they did not leave the boundaries of the light thrown out from the house. I continued on the lane. The dogs waited on the lawn of their home, once again silhouetted against the light.

From down the road came a set of headlights and a rumble of a big truck engine. The dogs remained silent until the vehicle turned onto the lane, and then they began a barrage of barking that would have sent any stranger running. I spoke to them softly, telling them it was okay and that I knew who this was. Remarkably, they hushed. I flashed the beam of the flashlight to show the driver of the truck where I stood. The dogs remained quiet, watching, as the truck pulled up next to me and stopped. It was Mr. Lloyd. I was never so happy to see someone that evening as I was to see him. We exchanged hellos.

"Where's your truck?" Mr. Lloyd asked.

I pointed down the lane. "It's pretty steep and sandy," I said. I don't know how we'll get it out of there."

"This truck will pull it out," he informed me confidently, patting his truck's door fondly. "I got about 50 foot of chain in the back. I'll drive down only as close as I need to and hook your truck to my truck with the chain and pull your truck outta there."

It sounded like a plan to me. We pulled the heavy chain out of his pickup. I could see the dogs pacing the yard. I wondered if they might start barking again or come down to where we were. They did neither. They seemed to understand they had no jurisdiction that far from their house.

We walked down to my truck, dragging the chain between us. Mr. Lloyd hooked the chain on the ball hitch of my truck, and we lined the chain out along the ground, up the lane toward his truck. He had tow hooks installed on the front of his truck, a huge one-ton 4-WD dually work truck. I sure hoped it wouldn't grind a trough beneath each of those double wheels and bury his axle, too.

"You get in your pickup, put it in neutral, take the brake off and just steer enough to keep it straight on the road," Mr. Lloyd said.

I nodded my understanding, and trotted to my truck and got in. He strode to his truck's door and got in, cranked the big engine, and began backing up slowly, bringing the slack out of the chain. The chain grew taut. I felt my pickup jerk in place. Mr. Lloyd's truck howled, and inched backward, spewing sand with the four big rear tires. I prayed he would not get stuck too. We didn't move. My pickup rolled back into its ruts as Mr. Lloyd eased up off the chain, put his truck in neutral, applied the emergency brake and got out.

I met him half way.

"Start your engine," he said. "You're pretty stuck there. It's going to take both engines to get you out of there. Put it in reverse and ease it back as I pull, okay?"

"Okay," I agreed. We went back to our respective vehicles.

This time, when Mr. Lloyd's truck had taken the slack out of the chain and begun to haul back, I put my truck in reverse and eased down on the accelerator. There was a moment of worry as the tires spun without gaining purchase, and then the truck lurched out of the rut, wheels spinning. Mr. Lloyd's truck backed up the hill, easily dragging my pickup. He didn't stop until we got both trucks on level, solid ground.

After removing the chains from between the vehicles, I told Mr. Lloyd to lead the way to his cow. He nodded, and headed out.

I looked over to the quiet dogs, and saluted them. "Thank you!" I said meaningfully. The silhouettes wagged their tails in acknowledgement. I got in my truck and took off after Mr. Lloyd's receding taillights.

About half a mile down the road, Mr. Lloyd's truck's taillights flashed and the truck took a sharp right turn off the Patterson Cemetery Road. This was the fork

I had missed in the dark. We traveled the dirt road about a quarter of a mile. Just after passing a set of pens that loomed out of the dark on the left-hand side of the road, the truck ahead of me flashed its tail lights again, turned to the left and stopped in front of a pipe gate. Mr. Lloyd got out and opened the gate, got in again, and drove into the pasture. I followed. The cow pens were just inside the gate on the road.

Flashlight in hand, I met Mr. Lloyd at the fence. In the pen stood a black Brangus cow, invisible in the moonless, starless night, but revealed to us in our flashlight beams. A dark brown, newborn calf was curled up at her feet. The cow blew her breath sharply at us.

"She's usually a real quiet cow," Mr. Lloyd said. "She's a little upset right now."

"Can't blame her," I said, shining my flashlight down her length. A large, irregular dark red blob was suspended from her rear end. It was definitely a prolapse, and definitely almost the entire uterus. However, from what I could deduce from the cow's behavior, we still had a good chance of saving the cow.

Mr. Lloyd went into the pen, cautious enough of the cow to stay near the fence, and shushed at the cow, causing her to move away from him and toward the alleyway at the end of the pen. She walked quietly down the chute to the head gate. I placed a bar behind her while Mr. Lloyd worked the head gate, trapping the cow's neck quickly in the gate. I went back to my truck for supplies.

A prolapse of the uterus is a very scary thing to see, especially to the uninformed. Mr. Lloyd had done the right thing by penning the cow and keeping her quiet until he got some help.

Normally the uterus begins a process called "involution" right after the calf and afterbirth have been delivered. During the calf's development, the uterus expands and enlarges from its pre-pregnancy size of about eight inches in length to an organ large enough and strong enough to contain a fully developed calf of from 50 to 80 pounds. Added to that is, of course, the placenta and all the fluids that go with the job of sheltering the calf in utero. Amazingly the involution process will shrink the entire uterus down to nearly the original, pre-conception size within 48 hours after parturition (calf delivery).

A prolapse of the uterus may occur after a difficult or prolonged delivery of a calf. Pain will cause the cow to continue to strain after the calf had been born. With the cervix wide open, the organ can turn inside out, coming out of the cow. If the blood supply is not interrupted, involution will still occur, although the organ usually cannot reduce fully while still inside-out on the outside of the cow. If the blood return from the uterus to the body is compromised, then the uterus cannot shrink, and will often continue to get larger. There is a grave danger of the cow injuring the uterus in her attempt to get up and move around, with hemorrhaging and death occurring. Some cows will continue to strain due to the pain of the prolapse, and may cause their intestinal organs to prolapse also. Undoubtedly when a cow has a prolapse, it's a very serious situation. Medical attention is needed as soon as possible.

Luckily, this cow was calm, and had not injured the everted organ. By flashlight illumination, I gave the cow an epidural in her sacral-coccygeal space. This would prevent her from straining against my efforts to replace the exposed uterus, and relieve her pain until the involution process had gotten under way.

If a prolapse is not tended as soon as possible after it occurs, the involution process will cause the cervix to constrict closed, making the return of the uterus to its home in the abdomen difficult and maybe impossible. Happily, this cow's cervix was still wide open. I was confident I could return the uterus to its correct place and restore the cow's health.

As I worked, I asked Mr. Lloyd about the family whose house I had trespassed into to get to the phone.

"You know, I don't know," he answered. "I've seen the kids, and all those dogs, but I don't know the people's name."

"Where were they?" I asked, as I cleaned up the brick red uterus with a mild soap and water. "Any idea? There was no one home, except the dogs. And all those vehicles in the yard. What happened to them?"

Mr. Lloyd appeared to dwell on the question. "I bet I know," he finally said, smiling with his voice out of the dark. "They have kids, right?"

"Right," I said, starting the process of easing the prolapse back into its rightful place inside the cow. "Looked like grade school, from the book bags in the hallway."

He chuckled. "I'll bet the other vehicles belong to other parents with kids. I'll bet you a dime to a dollar they all sat down to dinner, and had to get up and run off to a ball game or something. I know the mother drives a minivan. Bet they all piled into it and took off; kids, parents and all. Everyone except the dogs."

It sounded likely. "I checked the bedrooms," I confessed. "No dead bodies anywhere." Mr. Lloyd gave a short bark of laughter. "You're probably right."

I finished with the cow. She was a little wobbly in the rear from the epidural, but once released from the chute, she made her way back across the lot to her calf, where she eased herself to the ground to rest. I was sure she'd be all right now.

I cleaned up my equipment and stowed it in my truck. Mr. Lloyd got out his checkbook.

"Tell you what," he said. "When I come down here in the morning to check on this cow, I'll stop over and check on that family, too. It's about time I introduced myself to them; we are neighbors, after all. I'll call your office, let you know what I find out."

"That would be wonderful," I said gratefully. "It was sure a spooky thing, going in a house like that and everything set for dinner, the food half eaten, and no one there. Real scary."

Mr. Lloyd did call me in the morning to tell me he had stopped in to meet his neighbors the Hopewells. There were the parents, two grade school children and seven dogs. He said the dogs wouldn't let him out of his truck, and barked continuously and fiercely until Mrs. Hopewell came out of the house and walked out to his truck to see what he wanted. Nice people, he said, but fierce dogs, every one of them. The Rottweiler could sure bark, but he was most worried about the ankle-biting Dachshund, and never did get out of his truck while there. He did not tell her I had gone into the house to use the phone; he didn't want to worry her with that detail.

❋

Mr. Lloyd's cow recovered and raised her calf with no further problems. There was little routine about that particular call-out. I'll never forget that pack of dogs and the way they allowed me onto their territory and into their home that dark night. I thought about it many times in the years that followed. It had to be another case of the ability of animals to read the true intent of a human being, but also that of the powers that be once again helped me out of a fix.

Chapter Four

Mr. Swanson's Lame Bull

Animals can communicate quite well. And they do. And generally speaking, they are ignored. ~Alice Walker

Unlike dogs, which are often considered highly intelligent by their people, cows are often thought of as mindless creatures whose job it is to graze, give milk, and supply meat for steaks and hamburgers. While they do graze, give milk, and most of them do eventually end up as protein on our dinner plates, cows are far from mindless.

Every cow, bull or steer has its own personality, its

own take on the world. One of the things I learned while dealing with cattle is how to read their body language a little bit better, that of both cattle and people. Cattle are experts at reading the body language of humans, whether or not most humans are even aware of the cows watching them. Cattle are, after all, prey animals, and as such must constantly be aware of every little movement made in their surroundings. The size of the animal doesn't matter, either. Grown bulls can be just as leery of strangers as are smaller cows or calves. They do not wish to end up providing humans with a meal any sooner than they absolutely have to, either.

A call one morning came in from a rancher whose cows I had seen a couple of times. The pens and chutes of this particular ranch were very poorly constructed of faulty design and materials. The times I had driven up to see chutes like that, my inclination was to immediately rope the cow and work with her tied to a tree or stout post, rather than chance the cow smashing through the frail network of pens to freedom. This time, the rancher had a bull with a lame foot. I suggested he might want to bring the bull to the clinic, rather than have me come to his ranch, knowing as I did the condition of his chutes. Mr. Swanson assured me that the bull in question was gentle, having been halter-broke as a calf and would lead like a puppy on a string. So, with doubts, I agreed to drive out to see the bull on his home turf.

The first thing I noted on arrival at the ranch was the condition of the pens. They were shabbier than I remembered. To really draw attention to their dilapidated state, in the crowding pen was an enormous gray Brahman bull. The hump on his back cleared the top board of the sagging fence by what looked like three feet. He had an enormous head, upon which sat huge, swept back horns above thick, heavy brows that almost obliterated his tiny eyes. He had his left rear foot cocked, delicately balanced on one toe, indicating pain in that foot. I got out of my truck, and stood by the relative safety of its red bulk, eyeing the bull with a large amount of awe and trepidation.

Mr. Swanson came out of his house and crossed the yard to the pens. He was a small man, probably in his late 60s or early 70s, and wheezing from emphysema. He was attempting to untangle a small, ratty rope that didn't look like it could restrain a Chihuahua, much less a full-grown Brahman bull. I hoped he didn't intend to rope the bull with it. Mr. Swanson coughed once or twice into his handkerchief, and pointed to the swollen left rear leg of the bull.

"Been like that about three days," he said slowly. "He's pretty lame."

That much was obvious. I was going to have to look closely at the foot, to determine the reason for the pain and swelling. That meant restraining the bull in some manner. I sure didn't like the condition of the pens, though, especially with such a big bull.

"I can walk up to him," Mr. Swanson informed me. "He's real gentle. He's used to being handled." However, I noticed that Mr. Swanson did not move to approach the bull, but stood next to me, fiddling with the sorry little rope in his hands.

"We'd better see if he'll go down the chute," I said. "I

will probably have to pick up the foot, look for nails or something."

"Looks like foot rot to me," Mr. Swanson offered. "Maybe you can just give me something to squirt on that bad foot."

"First we have to look at the foot," I replied. "It won't do any good to put something on the outside, if there's a nail inside." Mr. Swanson shrugged as if in partial agreement.

We held our positions, shuffling foot to foot for a few seconds more as we observed the bull. It looked like it was going to be me who would have to suggest to the bull he needed to go down the rickety chute. There was no way the sagging fence was going to allow me to climb it. The gate was made of barbed wire tied shut with an assortment of baling wire, hay string, and a little bit of spit. I decided I was going to have to separate the fence wires and crawl through the loose wire to the other side. So I did.

When I straightened up on the inside of the pen, the bull was still standing stock still, the wounded foot cocked ever so slightly. He was staring over the opposite fence, out toward his cows in the pasture. I wondered if he would jump the fence, or, because of his hurt foot, simply smash through the flimsy barrier and head out to pasture. Slowly, I took a step toward him.

He swung his massive head around to his flank in my direction and fixed his bright little beady eyes on my suddenly wide, very frightened eyes. He dropped his head a notch, never moving his eyes from mine, and blew out from his nostrils a long, loud exhalation of breath that promised trouble if I got even a tiny bit closer to him. He wasn't going to move, and he had requested, in not-so-subtle bovine language, that I should keep my distance. I swallowed. Could I bluff a lame bull, especially a 2000-pound lame bull, into moving away from me? I took a half a step toward him.

While my foot was still suspended in mid-stride, the bull did a half turn on the forehand, swinging his huge body around to face me head on, flicked his tail once, so the switch of it lay over his hip, and dropped his head just one notch lower. Then he raised a forefoot and with his massive cloven hoof, slowly drew a line in the dirt of the pen.

I gulped. I can take a hint. With barely a falter, I swung my advanced foot back behind me, and took a step backwards. The bull unhurriedly shook his head at me, causing a loop of saliva hanging from his mouth to slowly flip up and over his muzzle. I took another cautious step back, keeping my eye on the bull. Satisfied that his message was received, the bull raised his head, eyed me carefully to be sure I was retreating, and turned away. He flipped his long ears back in the direction of the pasture and resumed watching his herd of cows.

I crawled out of the pen, unhooking the fence barbs from my clothing as I struggled through the rusty wire, and stood up, shaking slightly, next to Mr. Swanson. "I don't think I'm going to be able to look at his foot," I said, pointlessly.

Mr. Swanson smiled gently.

"Tell you what we'll do," I continued, hemming a little as I cleared my throat. "I'll leave a squirt bottle with some medicine in it. If you can get next to the bull, like you say you can, try putting a little on the foot, between the claws, twice a day; see if that helps. If it doesn't, you might have to get him in a trailer, and bring him to the clinic."

Mr. Swanson nodded in agreement. I rummaged around in the truck, found the medicine I was searching for, and gave the bottle to Mr. Swanson. With just a moment of hesitation, he went back to the pen and crawled through the wire. I was afraid to watch. He walked slowly up to where his bull stood facing the pasture. The bull appeared to be ignoring the slight human coming up on his side. Mr. Swanson patted the bull firmly on the massive left shoulder. The bull flicked his left ear backwards at him, once. Mr. Swanson loosened the nozzle of the bottle, took careful aim at the bull's sore rear hoof and squeezed the medicine bottle, sending a stream of liquid toward the wounded foot of the bull. The animal stepped sideways away from the man, swung his head toward Mr. Swanson, snorted in annoyance, then calmly returned his gaze to the cows in the distance. I was astonished.

✳

Three days later Mr. Swanson called to tell me the bull was no longer lame. Apparently, it had been a mild case of foot rot and not a nail that had caused the lameness. Nevertheless, the bull's acceptance of the owner's familiar presence and the way he allowed the man to medicate that very sore foot was what had utterly amazed me.

CHAPTER FIVE

IT COULD HAVE BEEN RABIES

There is no fundamental difference between man and the higher animals in their mental faculties. The lower animals, like man, manifestly feel pleasure and pain, happiness, and misery. ~Charles Darwin

Just because you try to handle every cow with gentleness and respect doesn't always mean the cow will respond in kind. A cow that had been brutalized in the past might have a hard time accepting a change in handling technique. Or it may be a cow under the influence of a disease process having a hard time understanding much in her little cow brain. For instance, a condition commonly known as "grass tetany" affects a cow's ability to handle stress. Grass tetany is considered to be a magnesium deficiency. It is seen during certain seasons of the year and its development depends on certain weather conditions as well as feed intake for the cow. Also called grass staggers, a cow with the disease shows signs that include incoordination, irritability, and convulsions. She might appear to forget who her usual handler is, and is hypersensitive, belligerent, and defensive. She may also have a tendency to fight, may bellow, charge, and, if able to keep her feet under herself, may probably try to knock down and gore whoever comes near her.

Such was a case one fall day. Mr. Edwards, the rancher who called on me, was relatively new to the business of keeping cattle. He had a cow acting odd, he said. She was a nice young cow, one he had raised from a calf, and one who would eat from his hand and enjoyed having her neck scratched. Now she was trying to attack him, he said, and had frothy white saliva dripping from her mouth. He was alarmed by his normally placid cow's belligerent behavior and was worried that the cow might have rabies. Although rabies is always a possibility in any warm-blooded animal, the higher probability was that grass tetany was the cause of the cow's sudden change of behavior. I suggested to Mr. Edwards that he stay away from the cow and not aggravate her. Let me get out there and get a good look at her and we'd go from there.

Luckily for all parties involved, the cow had staggered into a good pipe corral and fallen to the ground, giving the owner time to close the gate on her. When I arrived at the ranch, the cow, a large black Brangus type, was in the pen lying near a large mud puddle, her eyes wide and unblinking, her head trembling, slobber trailing from her mouth. When she heard our voices, talking as we surveyed the cow from the safe side of the fence, her head whipped around in our direction and she sucked in her breath, opened her mouth wide and emitted a quavering bawl. The trembling of her head increased as she tried to keep her eyes focused on us. She attempted to lunge to her feet, gained them shakily, and charged at us, bellowing and slinging slobber.

Mr. Edwards and I stepped back from the pipe fence, thankful for the two-inch diameter iron rails of the fence between the cow and us. If ever a cow displayed all the symptoms of rabies, this one did. She looked for all the world exactly like the cow in an old black-and-white film we were shown in veterinary school of a cow gone mad from the rabies virus. While that differential was on my list of possible diagnoses that I named off for the owner, grass tetany was still number one on my list of causes for her behavior. Bearing in mind that a brain-addled cow was a brain-addled cow and capable of doing grievous bodily harm regardless of what was addling her brain, my next dilemma was how to restrain the cow for treatment purposes.

Getting the cow to come in close enough to rope was not going to be the problem. She was practically crawling up the fence to get at us. She had no horns; therefore, I'd have to rope her around the neck. As she bellowed and flung her wobbling body at us one more time, I dropped my lariat noose around her neck and took a wrap of the rope around a post in front of the cow and another wrap about ten feet down the rail, out of harm's way of the cow, and tied it off.

Now the cow was getting seriously angry. I had to quickly get a halter on her so I could loosen the rope on her neck, which was threatening to strangle the fighting cow. Mr. Edwards was nervous and inexperienced with dealing with such fury in a cow. I was able to get the halter on her in record time and without injury, which was quite the trick with this cow so intent on killing me. Once the halter was in place, I tied the halter rope up high on the fence and loosened the neck rope.

All this time, Mr. Edwards was standing back from the action, wringing his hands, his eyes huge, and staring in disbelief at his formerly gentle cow's wild behavior. He was thoroughly convinced that rabies was the sure enough cause of this change in the cow. I still didn't consider rabies as the number one diagnosis, and was fervently praying I was right in that thought.

Once the rope was secure, the cow became still, glaring at me as I leaned over the fence's top rail above her. She was trembling from nose to tail; her tail whipping back and forth in fury. I had to decide next on how to dose her with a remedy to counteract the hypo-magnesium state I hoped she was in.

The standard treatment for an active case of grass tetany was an intravenous solution containing the magnesium along with the other minerals of calcium, phosphorous, and potassium. However, I couldn't see myself getting cozy enough with this cow to try to get a three-inch long, 14-gauge needle into her jugular vein. I liked living too much.

A recent development at that time in veterinary medical treatments was an oral paste containing all the minerals that the intravenous product contained. Its intended use was for mild cases where the patient was cooperative and easily restrained. This cow was not on the label.

Looking at my enraged patient, I hesitated only for a moment before deciding to try the paste. It would be a lot easier and safer to inject a paste into this cow's mouth than to crawl in bedside with her to give an IV. Maybe it would work well enough to take the edge off the cow's condition so I could then place an IV line, if needed. After locating the tube of medication in my truck, I placed the large cylindrical tube of paste medicine into a dispenser gun and cautiously climbed back up on the top rail of the iron pipe fence so that I was once again above the tied-up cow.

The cow was still only briefly. Immediately upon seeing me lean out over the top of the fence, she bellowed loudly, her mouth wide open as she lunged toward me. I put faith in the fence to hold me and in the rope to hold the cow, and I aimed the tip of the paste gun into the gaping pink mouth and fired the paste, rapidly squeezing the trigger, effectively dumping the entire contents of the paste tube into the cow's oral cavity. I dropped down and jumped back from the fence. The cow was cursing me from her side of the fence, flinging herself side to side. I withdrew to stand next to Mr. Edwards, who stood a safe distance back from the fence and the furious cow.

"I'm not sure if this will work," I said. "It might take a while."

"What if she's got rabies?" asked the rancher, casting a sidelong glance at me while keeping his main focus on his agitated cow.

I pondered the question. I wasn't at all sure how long she would live if it actually was the deadly virus acting on her mental workings that might have caused this display of symptoms.

"She'll die," I said. "But I don't know how long it will take. Maybe a couple more days."

We stood solemnly studying the cow. "If it is rabies," Mr. Edwards asked, nervously studying the cow, "what do we do after she dies?"

I slowly wiped some cow slobber off my hands. I had been exposed to rabies once before, while working as a technician, and had had to take the full series of shots to prevent infection. Though the treatment had changed over the years, it was still no picnic to have to endure. Rabies infection was inevitably fatal, however, and there was no other real option to stop infection besides the preventative injections if exposure to the virus had occurred.

"First, after she dies, we'd have to take her brain out, have it checked for the rabies virus," I told the man, and in my mind's eye I saw the brutal procedure of removing an animal's brain. With a large animal such as a cow, such a job is butchery at its worse. I did not look forward to it. "If she tests positive, the state will get involved with the quarantine and vaccination process for you and the animals that have been pastured with her."

Mr. Edwards groaned out loud. I could tell he regretted having called a veterinarian out to see the sick cow. A thought suddenly occurred to me. I turned to him.

"Are you worried about getting rabies from her?" I asked. "Because to get it you have to have been bitten or otherwise had exposure to her saliva." I studied the man carefully. He shifted his weight nervously and cast worried eyes in my direction.

"Did she bite you?" I was wondering how he might have gotten in a position to get bitten by a cow.

"She didn't attack me, if that's what you mean," Mr. Edwards said. "I thought maybe she had a stick in her mouth because she was foaming so much, and wouldn't take any cubes from me." He gestured weakly toward the cow. "She wasn't so upset then, not acting so... crazy. So I reached in her mouth, looking for a stick. She kind of bit me." He pulled off the left glove of the pair of leather gloves he wore, grimacing as he did so, and showed me the hand it had enclosed. I winched when I saw the bloody, crushed index finger, still raw from the trauma from the cow's molars. It sure looked painful.

I mulled the information over. Having a human exposed to a possibly rabid animal was a lot more serious problem than a cow with grass tetany. I was debating whether to suggest euthanatizing the cow right then and now and sending her brain off for testing, when I noticed a change in the rancher's position.

He was leaning forward toward the pen, intently watching the cow through the pipe rails. The look of consternation on his face had changed, becoming one of wonderment. "Doc?" he asked softly. "Does that cow look quieter to you?"

I turned to look, and indeed she did. She was no longer trembling. Her tail was still, except for an occasional swipe at flies. Her eyes, protruding and showing the whites in her fury at us earlier, had settled peacefully into their sockets, allowing her eyelids to close down and hide the white portion of the eyeball, giving her that gentle, bovine look.

"If it were rabies, she wouldn't get better from the medicine," I told Mr. Edwards. "Let's see what she does when we go up to her."

He held his ground only long enough for me to get a head start. We approached the cow, as close as the fence would allow. The cow watched us benignly. She rolled her tongue up over her nose, snorted gently, and regarded us kindly.

"I think the medicine worked," I said carefully. "It was grass tetany. She's going to be alright."

The change in the cow was like night and day. She was once again the gentle black mamma cow the rancher had raised from a calf. However, rabies being the strange, unpredictable disease that it is, I stopped Mr. Edwards as he reached out to stroke the cow's head.

"Let's do this," I said. "Let's take off the halter, but leave her in the pen for ten days. If she gets sick again, we'll be able to treat her more easily. If she dies, we'll have to remove the brain to check for rabies."

The man withdrew his hand from the cow's head hastily. It sounded like a plan to him.

I climbed up on the fence and reached over, tentatively testing the cow's response to my nearness. She snuffled my hand, her ears forward and interested, eyes calm and quiet. I loosened the halter quickly and slid it off her head. The cow gave a quick fling of her head and turned away, ambled to the water trough and drank, long and deeply. I heard Mr. Edwards heave a mighty sigh of relief.

"That's a good sign, isn't it?" he asked hopefully. "Her drinkin' water like that?"

"Excellent sign," I said, also encouraged by seeing the formerly deranged cow behaving with grace and dignity. "A very excellent sign."

✳

It was unquestionably the most rapid and dramatic response to treatment of grass tetany I had ever seen. The cow did not relapse into her former state of illness but, with proper feed and mineral supplements, returned to her normal self. Ten days later the owner released the fit, healthy and gentle cow back into his pasture.

CHAPTER SIX

The Cow with the Very Sharp Horns

Holy Cow! ~Harry Caray

Since so many diseases that can affect the brain adversely can also mimic an array of harmful symptoms in an animal, it's often a challenge to come up with the real reason for an animal's altered behavior. Besides viral infections such as rabies, there may be bacterial diseases or chemical imbalances like grass tetany. Anything causing a fever of high temperatures can cause symptoms of dementia, resulting in a normally placid beast going on a rampage. Mr. Fred Porter's cow was such a case, and she was very nearly the last cow I would have to examine.

Mr. Porter called my office one beautiful autumn Saturday due to a problem with a cow. The Porters had a weekend ranch in Pemberton, a small town about 25 miles from Crockett. Weekenders, as we called the folks who had permanent homes elsewhere and visited their ranches on weekends and holidays, comprised a substantial number of my clientele, and I was always happy to help them out. The Porters were among my favorites.

"She must have had her calf last weekend," Mr. Porter reported to me. "We live in Dallas, as you know, and only come down on weekends. She's an older cow, has had lots of calves. She was in labor when we left last weekend, but we didn't worry about her, as she had never had a calving problem before. But today she's looking bad. She's acting a little crazy and she's lost a lot of weight. Looks like afterbirth or something hanging out of her. We found the calf. He's alive, but he's pretty puny, like he hasn't nursed much," he finished. I told him I'd be along directly.

My assistant Leslie wanted to go along with me on the call. She was a good hand, so I told her to jump in the pickup. Off we went to the little township of Pemberton to see Mr. Porter's sick cow.

When we arrived at the modest ranch, Mr. Porter had the cow in his good wood board pen. The pen was muddy from the past week's rains and the cow had churned up the ground in the enclosure considerably while going around and around, seeking to escape. She was thin in comparison to the other cows that watched the proceedings from the pasture side of the fence. The cow in the pen had her head up, her eyes showed white, and she was snorting loudly through her distended nostrils as she ran along the fence line. She stank badly from the rotting rope of what appeared to be afterbirth dangling from her vagina. Her udder was flabby and did not appear to be producing milk. The calf was lying down in another pen, separated from the cow; she paid him no mind as she sought to escape the confinement of the pen.

We checked on the calf first. He was still alive, but obviously undernourished and weak. My guess was the cow was running a fever from the infection due to the retained afterbirth. Fever can cause a serious reduction in milk production as well as weight loss. The calf was simply not getting enough nourishment from his sick mother. We had to get the cow cleaned up, the afterbirth removed, and the cow on antibiotics. Once her fever was down and the infection under control, the cow would be able to resume producing milk for her calf. The first trick, though, was getting the cow into the chute and restrained in the head gate so I could work on her in relative safety.

Besides being a little crazed from the fever she undoubtedly had, what made this cow particularly tricky to work with were her horns. Each horn was easily 18 inches in length, and had grown to the side before growing forward from her head. They had wickedly pointed tips that almost twinkled in the afternoon sun. The cow knew, exactly to the millimeter, the length of each of those horns. She raked them along the fence as she trotted back and forth, shook them menacingly at us as we neared the fence, and otherwise indicated she was well aware of the weaponry she carried on her head. She knew she had us intimidated.

Most cattle pens have a large gathering corral, into which the cows are herded from the pasture. From this corral the cows can be directed into a smaller crowding pen, usually attached to a chute. The chute directs the cattle to a head gate in which the cows, one at a time, are caught around the neck to restrain them for whatever procedure is necessary, be it branding, vaccinations, deworming, or other medical treatment.

This cow did not want to enter the crowding pen. Each time she came around the larger corral, she would veer away from the entrance to the smaller pen. The big 12-foot gate was wide open, but she refused to go through it. I was worried the cow would overheat or otherwise over-stress herself if she continued to careen around the big corral.

Mr. Porter had long, lightweight bamboo poles to help direct cattle in the pens from the relative safety of the top board of the surrounding fence. He and I each took a pole, climbed up the sides of the fence and attempted to use the long poles to try to steer the cow toward the crowding pen. The cow would have none of it and simply tossed the poles aside with a flick of her horns, and continue to charge around the corral.

My mission was the save the cow and along with her, the calf. The cow did not understand why she was cornered, in pain, and separated from her calf. She only knew she wanted out of the corral. However, there was nothing I could do for her until I could get my hands on her. She had to go into the crowding pen and down that chute to the head gate if I was to help her.

We had the gate to the pen open wide, to entice the cow to enter. She refused turn after turn around the corral to be directed into it. At one point, she tossed her head and caught the nice, long pole I had in my hands, jerking it out of my hands and causing it to fly up and away, into the center of the muddy corral where it stuck, straight up, in the wet ground.

It was a good, stout pole. I wanted it back.

As the cow charged to the other end of the corral, I slipped down the fence boards into the corral. My booted feet sank six inches into the mud. Leslie and Mr. Porter warned me to be careful. I was fairly young, fairly agile, and, in this case, fairly stupid. I didn't see a problem with what I was doing. I waded through the mud toward the pole I wanted to retrieve.

As I leaned toward the pole to pull it from the mud, I saw the cow throw her head in my direction. She snorted loudly, dropped her horned head, and charged across the corral toward me, the mud making loud sucking noises as it pulled at her cloven hooves, slowing her advance somewhat. I turned to run to the fence; confident I would make it with time to spare. However, the same mud slowing the cow down also had a firm grip on my rubber boots. A thrill of panic shot up my spine as I fought to pull my feet loose from the mud. One foot slid out of its boot just as I got a hand on the board fence. I tried to pull my other foot loose with Leslie and Mr. Porter hollering at me to hurry up.

Everything suddenly seemed to enter a time warp. Things were moving slowly; the pulling of one foot from its stuck boot, the grabbing on the fence, and the climbing attempt while one boot, with foot, remained firmly stuck in the mud. Everything was slow except the charge of the cow. In a split second she was upon me, bawling, saliva flinging from her mouth, her head down, and those twinkling horns aimed right for the small of my back.

I turned around to face the oncoming cow, one foot on the fence, the other foot still in its boot, still firmly planted in the mud, twisting my knee. I could hear both Leslie and Mr. Porter screaming, reaching for me from the other side of the fence. All I could see, though, was that approaching cow, those wicked horns leveled at my midsection.

I was going to die. On this pretty fall day in a muddy cow pen, I was going to die by being gored in the belly by a sick cow. I couldn't get my foot out of its mud-trapped boot so I could climb the fence to safety. I had turned completely around to face my executioner, back to the fence.

And that cow hit, hard, her head centered right on my abdomen. The board fence behind me vibrated from the impact. I was screaming, or at least I was emitting a high-pitched whine, waiting for the pain. I wondered why I couldn't feel the horns. It must have been the adrenalin surging through my system. The cow bellowed, her breath hot on my legs. I looked down at her, expecting to see blood gushing from around a horn embedded in my belly. What I saw was the top of the cow's head centered on my navel. She had missed me with her horns. Instead, she had hit the fence with her horns, one on each side of my waist. She had hit the fence so hard the horns had embedded in the wood, holding her fast. I was alive, unharmed but trapped between the fence and cow's forehead, a horn on each side on me.

It felt like a cartoon with none of the humor. My ears felt as though they were stuffed with cotton. Through my muffled ears I could hear Mr. Porter and Leslie hollering. I realized I was screaming too, above the bellowing of the angry, fevered cow whose nose poured hot breath on my thighs, her body flailing as she angrily tried to push toward me and tried to do me grievous harm. The board at my back vibrated from the shaking the cow was giving it, first pushing toward me, then her pulling back, as she tried to pull her horns free of it. I worked at freeing my trapped foot from the half-buried mud boot.

I knew if I was going to stay in one piece, if I was going to live, I had to get up the fence and away from the cow. I couldn't turn around, as the fit between the fence and the cow's head was tight. I tried unsuccessfully to lever myself up between her horns, one hand on each horn. The cow tried to pull back, but she was stuck tight in the board. She flung her body from one side to the other, bellowing angrily. The board cracked, but still held.

I began to pound her on the poll of her head with my fist but all that did was make her angrier. I began to punch her nose with my right knee, bringing my leg up as hard as I could, over and over again. After about the third punch, it was evident to me the cow was trying to pull away, but her horns were still stuck solid in the boards behind me. I stopped thumping her nose with my knee. Panting from fear and exertion, I twisted my body at the waist just a little, and pulled myself up the railing, leaving the cow in the board and my boots in the mud.

I scrambled to the top of the fence just as the board splintered and the cow pulled herself free. She blew and hooked her horns upwards toward me a couple times before trotting off to the other end of the corral again. I was panting as if I had run a 50-mile race at full tilt. Leslie and Mr. Porter were excitedly asking me if I was all right, did she hurt me. They were beside me, patting my back, checking for blood.

"No, I'm fine," I assured them two or three times. My breathing and nerves calmed down, the cottony sensation in my ears dispersed, and I became aware of how frightened Leslie and Mr. Porter were from the looks on their faces, their rapid, scared intake and exhale of their own panting breaths. I turned to see where the cow was. She pacing along the other end of the corral.

"Good Lord, girl," Mr. Porter commented, an audible tremble in his voice. "I wasn't sure you were going to get out of there."

"Neither was I," I assured him. "My boots are wrecked, though. And I didn't get my stick back, either. It was a good stick, too."

Mr. Porter snorted a nervous laugh. "Well," he said. "You sure can keep your sense of humor."

What else could I do? There was no reason to get angry at the cow—she couldn't help how she was feeling. She stood at the other end of the pen, snorting, pawing the ground in frustration before starting her mad trot around the corral again. This time, however, instead of bypassing the gate to the crowding pen, she ran through it.

As she entered the smaller space, I jumped down, bootless, into the muddy corral and ran across the lot to swing the gate shut behind her. She hooked her horns at it once as it swung toward her, but did not attempt to escape. I retrieved my ruined boots from the mud, and pulled them back on. They were cold and uncomfortable and full of mud and cow manure. I didn't have another pair with me, so they would have to do. I looked around and saw the pole the cow had knocked from my hand. I pulled it from the mud, certain I would need it again.

The cow, once confined in the smaller pen, appeared to have accepted her capture. She calmed down, dropped her head, and slowed her respiration. With a little coaxing, she trotted into the chute leading to the head gate. As she stuck her head out the opening of the head gate, Mr. Porter deftly caught her. We would now be able to work on her. With Leslie's help, I got my equipment from my truck, hoping the tremors from my scare would subside enough for me to be able to do my work.

The first thing I did was get my thermometer out and take the cow's temperature. It was a burning 105 degrees. Normal for a cow is 101. This was a very sick cow.

The placenta, or afterbirth, was very rotted, smelled horrible, and required me to glove up and go into the cow to loosen it. It fell free from its uterine attachment with just a little effort. We then lavaged her uterus with a disinfectant solution, gave her medication to combat the infection and fever, and turned her out with her calf. Mr. Porter thought he could pen up another cow that was feeding her own calf, see if the calf would nurse the cow until the mother cow was again producing milk.

Leslie and I drove away from the ranch, leaving Mr. Porter to settle the cow in the pen with hay and water. He reported to us later that the cow's fever had disappeared after a couple of hours, and she had calmed down. Her udder filled with milk within 24 hours, and she was able to resume nursing her calf.

※

For me, this was one more unexpected adventure that came with what should have been a routine job. It was also another tough call out that proved to me once again that powers beyond my scope of understanding kept faithful watch on me as I did my duty.

CHAPTER SEVEN

HE SWEARS HE NEVER TOUCHED HER

Compassion for animals is intimately connected with good-ness of character; and it may be confidently asserted that he who is cruel to animals cannot be a good man.
~Arthur Schopenhauer (philosopher)

When I first opened my practice, any person calling for help with an animal could depend on my swift and eager response to tend to their animal's need. I had to learn the hard way that not all people were appreciative of my willingness to help. Those people made it hard for anyone to want to work for them. Leo Grady was one such person.

I'd already taken my shower and was getting ready for bed one Saturday night when the phone rang. Telephones chiming at such a late hour can make any veterinarian quiver in fear and frustration. I tentatively picked up the receiver and answered the call.

A gruff, older gentleman's voice boomed into my ear. "I need to talk to the vet!" he shouted. After confirming that I was indeed the veterinarian and not the veterinarian's wife, I politely asked who was calling. Instead of answering that question, the man grumbled some remark about women doing men's work, and impatiently asked was how much would it cost for me to come to his place to deliver a calf. Looking at the clock, I saw the time stood at the 10:00 hour. I told him there would be an after hours call as well as a regular call charge.

"All you vets care about is money!" he snorted righteously into my ear. I ignored that comment and asked him where the cow was.

"In the pen at my place!" the man almost shouted at me. I held the receiver out from my ear. He had yet to identify himself. Since I still had no idea who I was on the phone with, I again asked him for his name and where his place was located.

"Grady! Leo Grady! In Singleton! Up by the Hyle ranch!" He was shouting now, sounding very agitated.

I was fairly new to the area. I did know where Singleton was, but had never heard of the Hyle ranch.

"The what ranch?" I asked after writing his name down on my message pad.

"HYLE! The Hyle Ranch! Up near Singleton Lake!"

At this point in my career I had been in Crockett

maybe four months. Besides not recognizing the Hyle Ranch name, I did not know who this thundering Leo Grady might be. I did get the impression he was a short-tempered rancher who had been unable to raise another veterinarian on this warm summer night. He obviously wasn't keen on spending a lot of money on a cow in labor, either. Most seasoned veterinarians will use just about any excuse to get out of assisting such a client, especially at such an inconvenient hour of the night.

Here it was, 10:00 pm, and I was on the telephone, in a bathroom robe and fresh out of the shower, a towel wrapped around my wet hair, being yelled at by a total stranger. I didn't like such rudeness and considered simply hanging up. However, even after such a short time in veterinary medicine, I knew many people would take out their fear and frustration on the veterinarian when feeling helpless over the condition of one of their animals. Wondering what I was getting into, I told Mr. Grady in as calm a voice as I could muster that I was new to the area and not familiar with the Hyle Ranch or where it was.

"Well, how much will it cost for you to come out here?" he bellowed irritably again.

By this time I had unfolded the county map, holding the phone to my ear as I searched the map for Singleton Lake. I found the small body of water on the map quickly. I told Mr. Grady the distance to his ranch would determine the cost of the call-out and there would be a night emergency call charge as well. The calf delivery charge would be determined by the time and effort it took to accomplish the task.

Mr. Grady fumed and sputtered over the line, muttering about cows not being worth the money spent on them, and veterinarians being worth even less. I got the impression he might continue along this vein half the night. I gave him a few minutes to vent his anger before I finally asked him point blank if he wanted me to come or not. He stopped his ranting for a moment before reluctantly saying yes, he wanted me to make the call out. In an irritated and loud voice, he gave me directions to his ranch.

My husband, Jack, had come into the room while I was still holding the phone, listening to Mr. Grady continued to rant at me. Jack had been able to hear the man's angry voice, and had listened to my end of the exchange. He knew without asking that I would be going out that night to a place I'd never been, to face an angry man I had never met. Without any trouble at all he had picked up on the rancher's unfriendly nature. He asked me if I wanted him to go along on the call. I said yes, gratefully.

I got dressed, pinned my freshly washed and still damp hair up on my head, and covered it with a bandana to protect it from the mess that accompanies a calf delivery. I filled a couple gallon jugs with hot water and checked the other supplies in the truck. Map in hand, we headed out into unknown territory.

Mr. Grady's ranch was about 15 miles from Crockett. The Hyle Ranch sign, a landmark Mr. Grady had given me, was located out by the highway. It was unlit, but we found it easily enough as it was large and painted white with black letters easily picked out of the darkness by my truck's headlights. I steered the truck down the dirt road next to the sign, as indicated in our directions. As Jack navigated, we weaved along the back roads of north Houston County, following the directions given, looking for a white pickup truck parked alongside one of the side roads. Finally, up ahead was a white pickup, sitting facing up another dirt road. As we approached, the pickup's door opened, causing its cab lights to come on. A large, big bellied man, presumably Mr. Grady, climbed off the driver's seat, and stalked over to my window as I pulled up behind his truck.

"Took ya long enough to get here!" he snarled, red-faced in the glow of my cab's overhead light. I was taken aback, but before I could comment, he continued barking at me. "We gotta go down this road a bit to get to my pasture," he snapped. "Follow me so you don't get lost again!" He turned and strode back to his own truck, climbed in and slammed the door to the cab violently.

"What an asshole," my husband observed dryly. "Is that the guy who called?"

"I guess," I answered. "Same mean voice."

"Why are you going to help him?" Jack asked. "He's a butt."

"He's got a cow in trouble," I shrugged.

Ahead of us, Mr. Grady's truck jerked to a start and roared away up the side road. We followed. After bumping down the dirt lane for a short distance, the white pickup turned off the road and jerked to a halt. Mr. Grady got out. Without a backwards glance toward us, he lumbered to a gate in the road, threw it open, climbed back into his truck, and roared into the pasture. Jack and I looked at each other, shrugged, and followed. I stopped my pickup inside the gate and Jack jumped out to shut it. By the time Jack got back into his seat, Mr. Grady's truck had just about disappeared into the dark. Luckily, its white paint and flashing tail lights made it a little easier to track in the dark. I was happy Jack was with me. I had no idea what Mr. Grady's behavior would be like when we finally stood face to face.

We were led down a narrow, sandy path into the woods, the trees close on either side of us, until a board cattle pen loomed out of the darkness ahead of us. The white pickup shuddered to a halt beside the pen, and the driver emerged again from the vehicle. We pulled up next to him and got out.

"Mr. Grady?" I asked, as I approached the obviously irritated and tight-lipped man. He nodded once, ignoring my extended right hand. After barely acknowledging my introduction to my husband and myself, he jerked his head to the left, toward the pen.

"Heifer's in the pen," he barked. "I found her this morning trying to calve. I put her in this pen, *and all I did was watch her all day*." His jaw ruminated. "Seemed like she wasn't going to have that calf without help, and it was gittin' late. I couldn't get no other vet out here. So, I had to call you. I hope this don't take all night. I want to go home."

I had to wonder to myself why he waited all day to get help for the cow. Maybe he had tried earlier to get some assistance, but with his delightful demeanor, had dissuaded anyone else from agreeing to come out. I looked over the high board fence and shined my flashlight beam onto the white face of a small red heifer that was standing, quivering, on the other side of the pen. She dropped her head and snorted at me, shaking her little six-inch horns in warning. She looked tired, drawn, and big-bellied. I scouted out the pen and saw that a high-walled chute ran down the side of the pen on the right. There was no head gate, but I determined if we could run the heifer into the chute and put a bar behind her, she couldn't back out of the chute. I could examine her safely that way.

When I explained what I wanted to do, Mr. Grady acted put upon. He began grousing about cost again, about the value of the cow, and about all the vets who had refused to answer his calls earlier for help, so that he was stuck with a woman to help him. I could certainly understand why the vets familiar with this client might decline to return his calls. I clucked my tongue quietly and went ahead with my work.

The heifer weighed about 500 pounds; a rather small individual to be on the verge of delivering her first calf. An inquiry to the owner as to the type of bull she was bred to brought back the snapped answer of "Red Angus." He delivered a defensive tirade on the bull's suitability for first-time heifers, how none of his other cows had calving problems, and so on and so forth. His tirades were wearing on me. Still, the heifer needed help, so I set to the job.

The heifer was disinclined to enter the chute. She seemed determined to exit the pen by any means other than the chute. Due to her small size, large girth, and general weakness from a long day in labor, however, she was unable to climb, crawl, leap, or in any other way make her escape. She finally was enticed down the chute by me dropping down from the fence to land in front of her. This caused her to drop her horns and lunge toward me as I scurried ahead of her down the chute. I made my escape up the inside of the chute and over the top. Jack and Mr. Grady barred her ability to back out of the chute with long wooden posts inserted through the fence behind her. Mr. Grady never once stopped complaining about the expense and work to be done. I ignored him and continued to prepare to examine the heifer.

Because there was no head gate to restrain her, we had to get a rope halter on the heifer and tie her up. This was accomplished with the aid of flashlight illumination and luck. Once she was properly restrained, I climbed into the chute behind the pole that blocked an exit for her. Jack passed me a gallon of warm water, a couple of OB sleeves, and my disinfectant soap. I did a fast examination of the heifer's uterus.

In a normal calf delivery, the calf presents with its two front feet first, and the head following just about the level of the calf's knees. In this situation I found the calf to be dead, its two front feet set back behind the cow's pelvis, its head turned backwards. The calf did not feel too large for the heifer; it was just improperly positioned, making it impossible for the cow to deliver without assistance. Even the little manipulation I did during the exam caused the heifer's legs to buckle. We were going to have to let her back out of the chute, so we could tie her to a post in the pen. That way, if she fell down during the delivery, which she undoubtedly would, she would not become lodged in the narrow width of the chute, unable to get up again. It would also give me more room behind her to do my work.

Mr. Grady continued to complain bitterly about money as we allowed the heifer to move backwards slowly, careful to keep the halter rope tied around a stout post.

I explained to Mr. Grady what was going on with the heifer, how the calf was jammed tightly into the pelvic canal, and the fact that it might require some time and effort to remove. He swore loudly, saying he never had such problems, how he had watched the cow all day but never touched her. He complained how she wasn't worth the trouble and money, amongst other things. I wondered why I was there. Jack glanced at me and shrugged, as if he was thinking the same thing.

After lubricating my gloved hands and arms thoroughly, I went in search of the calf's front hooves.

Jack, holding the flash light in one hand and the cow's tail in the other, watched as I carefully reached in and searched around with my fingers. As I moved my hand around in the warm interior of the cow, I felt something a little out of place in a cow's uterus. Puzzled, I carefully grasped the object in my hand, and brought it out of the cow's vagina. What came out into the light turned out to be a long, orange hay string about a quarter of an inch in diameter. I held it up in the light so Jack could see it. Mr. Grady, griping away, was standing off to one side in the darkness and apparently did not see the string I had produced on my examination of the cow's insides. Jack made a knowing face in return of my grim smile at the string. In a loud stage whisper he asked, "WHY, IS THAT A HAY STRING YOU FOUND IN THAT COW?"

"I BELIEVE IT IS A HAYSTRING!" I answered just as loudly, grinning at my husband in amusement.

"NOW, HOW DID A HAY STRING GET INTO THIS COW?" Jack practically bellowed at me.

"WELL, I DON'T KNOW!" I replied, so loudly my vocal cords ached. "BUT THE STRING APPEARS TO BE TIED AROUND THE CALF'S LEG! OH, LOOK! THERE'S ANOTHER STRING ON THE OTHER LEG, TOO!"

Mr. Grady had gotten very still and quiet. Without looking in our direction and without another word he walked away from us, out the gate, and climbed into the cab of his truck, slamming the door so that the light ticked off and left him sitting in darkness. Jack and I grinned at each other. I went back to work. Obviously, in spite of his protestations to the contrary, Mr. Grady *had* tried to deliver the calf himself by using hay strings around the legs of the calf to provide some pulling traction. Unsuccessful with his own delivery attempt and rather than remove the strings, he had tucked the hay strings back into the cow, still on the legs of the calf, before calling in desperation for veterinary assistance.

With only the sounds of the cow's grunting breath, the crickets and night bird calls, Jack and I went to work to deliver the dead, wedged-in calf. It required the removal of the calf's head, but once that was done, I was able to bring the front legs into position, which allowed the remains of the small calf to exit fairly easily from the cow. The heifer was greatly fatigued and slipped to the ground to rest and gather her reserve strength while we cleaned up the equipment, medicated her against infection and pain, and put my tools back into the vet truck. As I washed my hands and arms of the smell and fluids from the heifer, Mr. Grady got out of his truck, check book in hand. He glanced once at the resting heifer before silently taking a pen from his shirt pocket to write the check out. He never offered a comment or indicated any displeasure at the price I quoted. He quickly wrote out the amount I requested, and thrust the check at me.

As I wrote the number of the check on his receipt, I told him the cow needed to rest a few minutes longer, before we would see if she could stand. I thought it best if she stayed in the pen for the night, with fresh water and some hay and feed to rebuild her strength.

Without acknowledging that he heard my advice, Mr. Grady stuffed his receipt in a pants pocket while walking over to the pen. He opened the gate and approached the heifer. She was still lying down, in sternal position. We had already removed the ropes restraining her. She swung her head back toward her owner, her eyes wide and glowing in the flashlight beam. She suddenly snorted angrily, and leapt with surprising agility and vigor to her feet. Mr. Grady stopped cold in his tracks in shock at her reaction to his presence. The little cow stood and faced him, suddenly dropped her horn-studded head, and feigned a charge at Mr. Grady.

The overweight rancher whirled around and, in an astounding burst of speed, took off out of the pen. The heifer was right behind him, her head lowered and the sound of her snorting breath filling the night air. She was so close to him he was unable to swing the gate shut behind him as he made his escape from the pen. He headed for his pickup, his big belly leading the way, his legs a blur as they pumped up and down in flight. The enraged heifer hooked her head toward the seat of his pants. He jumped, and, amazingly, was able to hoist himself up into the bed of his truck, out of harm's way. The heifer circled the truck, her little horns clanging on the metal of its sides as she hooked upward at the man, her tail whipping back and forth in fury.

Jack and I stood frozen next to my truck, watching this mini-circus by flashlight with amazement.

After deciding her quarry had escaped, the heifer swung toward Jack and me. A chill raced up my spine at the sudden danger. So intent on watching the cow chase the man, we had remained right next to my truck in a highly vulnerable position. We stood stock still with nowhere to run. The heifer slowed her approach and stopped. She appeared to appraise us carefully, then shook her head and pawed the ground once. Apparently, her opinion of us was not the same as the one she held for Mr. Grady, because she did not charge at us. She snorted once, then turned and trotted off, a slight wobble to her rear end, down the darkened path into the night.

When the clicking of her hooves on the path had faded in the distance, Mr. Grady carefully climbed down from the bed of his pickup. He got into the driver's seat without a word. He cranked the engine and backed his pickup away from the pen. We scurried into our truck and got the engine started and followed him back out the twisting lane in the woods to the main gate. At the gate, Mr. Grady pulled to one side and got out to hold the gate for us. I hollered "Goodnight!" as we drove past him, but he neither nodded nor acknowledged my exiting cry to him to have a Goodnight.

✳

Not surprisingly, Mr. Grady never called on me again, day or night. I really didn't care, as his sort made the work harder to do with just his presence. His check didn't bounce, either, so I was quite satisfied with the outcome of that late Saturday's work.

Chapter Eight

Born Alive!

The greatness of a nation and its moral progress can be judged the way its animals are treated. ~Mahatma Gandhi

After going on a few calf deliveries with me in which the fetus was already dead, my husband, Jack, was wondering if calves were ever born alive in Houston County. All the deliveries he had witnessed me perform were of dead calves, often putrid by the time veterinary services were called upon. Jack did not attend every calf delivery I went on, though, and I kept hoping one day he would come along on one and get to see a calf born alive and healthy.

One day a client, Herbert Weir, called and said his first-time heifer was trying to calve. Nothing was coming out but two feet. The heifer had not been in labor long, he claimed, and he could see the calf's feet wiggling a little. He was afraid the calf would die if not delivered soon and wanted me to come as quickly as possible.

It was a Sunday afternoon, so Jack was not at work. I asked him if he wanted to ride along, lend me a hand, and maybe get to see a live calf delivery. He agreed somewhat reluctantly to give it one more go.

The Weir homestead was far out in the country. We arrived to find the cow, a small but well fleshed Holstein, in a pen near Mr. Weir's house. She was standing up, was very alert and very unhappy to be penned up away from the other cows. From her vulva protruded two white calf feet, still draped in the amniotic sac. The calf to which the feet belonged was apparently still alive, as the two hooves showing outside the cow would jerk and wiggle as the cow shifted around the lot.

We roped and tied the cow to the nearest and safest fence post (not always the same thing on most of the farmsteads I visited). I gloved up while Jack helpfully got hold of the cow's tail to keep it out of my way. The calf was indeed alive but its nose was stuck under the brim of the cow's pelvis, preventing delivery. With a little manipulation, I was able to bring the muzzle up and over the pelvis of the cow, headed in the right direction. I put a chain on each foreleg, handing one chain handle to Jack while I kept one. We applied a little traction and a robust, black and white bull calf slithered easily out of his mamma and plopped onto the ground. He shook his wet ears and gave a lusty bawl at the world.

Jack was delighted. As I cleaned up my equipment

and repacked it into the truck, Jack marveled at the calf's long, wet floppy ears, the pink tongue sliding in and out of its mouth as the newborn wiped his own nose, and the heaving sides as the calf drew in the air of his new and much larger world. As the calf began to struggle to his feet, the new mother cow lowing and encouraging him with long licks of her rough tongue, Jack crowed with excitement. I was fascinated watching him watch the calf. He insisted that we stay on at the ranch for a while longer so he could watch the calf finally gain his unsteady legs and totter to the cow's udder for his first suckle.

During all of it, Mr. Weir said not a word. As he and I picked up and put away my equipment, I caught him casting a quick glance at Jack now and then. I think he might have viewed Jack as maybe a little eccentric, possibly even a little "touched." I finished putting away the cleaned equipment and joined Mr. Weir as he stood watching Jack coo over the calf.

Mr. Weir couldn't stand it anymore. He leaned over to me to get my attention. He cupped a hand around his mouth and whispered to me softly, "Ain't never seen a calf born, has he?" He watched Jack with the calf for a few seconds more before whispering to me again. "Cuz he sure is taken with that calf."

"He's only been on a couple of calf deliveries with me," I told him. "This is the first live one he's seen."

Mr. Weir drew back and smiled; he nodded in understanding. "Ah, the live ones," he said. "They's a miracle alright. Every last one."

I smiled back in agreement. Miracles indeed.

Chapter Nine

The Duvalls of Greenfield

We can judge the heart of a man by his treatment of his animals.
~Immanual Kant

Working with cattle meant, of course, working with the people who took care of them. For a number of my clients I never hesitated to respond to their calls for help. Word of mouth from appreciative clients led to other people calling on my service. And so my practice grew.

I came to have the Duvalls as clients by referral. They lived two counties over, near a small town called Greenfield. It was 56 miles from the clinic door to the Duvall's barnyard. Since most of my clientele were within 30 miles of the clinic, to have me drive almost twice that meant they must have liked my work.

Betty Duvall's father, Glen Bradley, Sr., known locally as Slim, lived in Houston County and was a regular client of mine and a regular visitor of the Duvalls. Slim told the Duvalls about me one day, after Betty had related to him their sad story of cow and calf losses in the preceding months. Apparently, they had called on their local veterinarians on seven different cases of dystocia, and had lost the seven cows along with their calves. Slim had informed them that I had been able to successfully deliver all the calves I was called out to the Bradley place to assist into the world. I don't recall if that was true or not, but in comparison with the deaths of seven cow-calf pairs, I might have sounded like a miracle worker to the Duvalls.
So, with her father's advice to use me as their cow vet, Betty Duvall called the clinic one cool spring day to ask me to come out. They had a two-year old Beefmaster heifer in labor. Their herd was all registered Beefmasters, and to lose still another cow to this problem was unbearable to them.

I didn't know what I was getting into. I did not know these people. They were well-established ranchers, but if their own veterinarian wasn't able to help the cows, how would I be able to? However, I was young, new to practice, and ready for the challenge. I agreed to drive the 56 miles to see what the problem was and decide if I could help the suffering cow. If I thought I could help the cow, I would stay at the ranch and do whatever was necessary to save the cow. I checked my truck for supplies, equipment, and fuel. I told my assistant, Leslie, to saddle up and come along to help.

I truly didn't know what to expect. Betty's family, my Houston County clients, the Bradleys, also ran a small cow operation. They used good cross-bred cows mated to quality Beefmaster bulls to produce fast growing calves for feed yards. The Bradley heifers tended to be well developed by the time they were turned in with a bull, and their calving problems were few. However, just because the Duvalls were related to the Bradleys by marriage didn't mean the Duvalls ran the same kind of operation. I wondered what condition the cows might be in. I almost expected to see runty heifers and huge bulls, to account for the deaths of seven cows and their calves from calving difficulties.

Due to the excellent directions given by Betty Duvall before we left the clinic that day, we were able to find the Duvall ranch—The Diamond D Ranch— without a single wrong turn down the back roads around Greenfield. The Diamond D pastures were thick with spring grass, and the cows observed from the road were big and fat. I followed the entry lane to the house, where we were met and greeted by a group of barking dogs, which surrounded my truck as soon as we entered the yard. A plump, sunburned woman, obviously alerted by her able crew of watchdogs, emerged from the house. She waded through the leaping dogs, attempting to stop the ones that jumped and bayed at my truck. I was disinclined to open the door.

"Mrs. Duvall?" I had opened my truck window a few inches and spoke to the owner over the roar of the dogs.

"Please call me Betty," she said. "You must be Dr. Cooper-Chase."

I rolled my window down further. We shook hands through the truck window solemnly. The dogs immediately began to grow quiet. It was as if they were willing to accept our presence based on Mrs. Duvall's welcoming handshake.

"Mr. Duvall's at the pens with the heifer," she told me, indicating the white pipe enclosure up the hill a little. "I'll follow you up on my four-wheeler, after I put the dogs up." She turned and hurried away, whistling and slapping her thighs to call the myriad dogs to her. They all turned from the truck and happily followed her, tails up and wagging, heading for their pen in the yard, having successfully done their proper duty of alerting against intruders.

I put the truck in gear, and followed the sandy path to the pens. Inside the first pen, sitting on an ATV, was an older gentleman who I assumed was Mr. Duvall. There were no dogs at the cattle pens. Leslie and I got out of the truck. The man waved me over to where he sat on the machine. I unlatched the gate, crossed through, and approached him.

I understood immediately upon meeting Mr. Duvall why he had to summon help to deal with problems like the one presented. I was also glad I had brought my assistant with me on this call. Though well muscled in his shoulders and arms, it was apparent the man was paralyzed below the waist. I never found out the cause of his infirmity, but over the following years I watched him work his cows from his ATV with all the finesse and ability of a cowboy mounted on a champion stock horse. However, getting off the machine and dealing with an individual case on the ground was not possible for him. I was to find out later that Betty Duvall was herself a fine cowhand, but reluctant to attempt assisting a cow in dystocia. I learned that they had two sons, neither one of whom lived in the immediate area, and were therefore unavailable to help out. Neither of their two grown daughters had an interest in the cows. So, when they had a problem with the cows, the Duvalls called on professionals. After this call-out, I was to become their veterinarian of choice, and they willingly paid me to make the long drive to their ranch when necessary.

This day, this first day I was to help out, they did not know me. They did not know if I would be any more helpful than the veterinarians employed in the last seven cases had been. Mr. Duvall was skeptical, without a doubt. He looked me up and down, trying to judge my capabilities by my appearance. I stood a hand taller than his wife, but weighed probably 30 pounds less. I'd seen the look a million times. It was a look that held a little disappointment, a little surprise, and a lot of doubt. I smiled, greeted him cheerfully, and shook his hand, then introduced Leslie to him.

His jaws were working a large wad of chewing tobacco, and a thin brown line of juice dribbled from the corner of his mouth. He spat a long brown stream into the dust of the lot, and indicated the cow lying in the pen before us.

She was a large, well-grown Beefmaster heifer. She sat up on her brisket, facing away from us. Her eyes held a tired, preoccupied look, and as Mr. Duvall explained what the problem was, the cow strained half-heartedly, her back bowing upward. A puddle of fluid, red-tinged, had formed in the dirt under her tail. A thick rope of tissue hung from her vulva and a foul smell permeated the country air. Flies buzzed around her noisily. From these pieces of evidence, before I ever touched the cow, I deduced the calf must already be dead.

"She's been in labor almost two days," Mr. Duvall stated, and quickly threw a hand into the air as if to stop me from voicing my outrage. "I called all the vets around here first," he continued. "They all made excuses why they couldn't come out. They had already killed seven of these good heifers. I guess they're sick of us." He spat again, in disgust, in silent fury. I didn't say a word, waited for him to go on. His jaw rotated as his ruminated on his chaw. "Slim says you can help us," he finished, sighing in resignation.

I shuffled my feet, a little embarrassed, a little afraid. What had Slim Bradley gotten me into? What had I gotten myself into? "We need to look at her first, Mr. Duvall," I said. "Can she get up?"

"She tried, but she couldn't last time we tried to get her up," he said, indicating a battery-powered cattle prod leaning up against the empty ATV seat next to him. "She ain't going nowhere."

I nodded, heading back to my truck for supplies, signaling Leslie to come help. I would first exam the cow, see how the calf was positioned, and what condition it was in. Then I would attempt to deliver the calf. From there I would be able to rate the cow's chances of recovery. I got my long plastic gloves, water,

soap, lubricant, and went into the pen with the cow.
Leslie had produced a lariat into which she built a loop
to drop over the cow's head. It was a precaution against
the cow getting up and leaving the area. Too many
cows that were rated as unable to get up were known
to suddenly leap to their feet and run when the work
began in earnest.

The heifer did not seem to notice us. She didn't
move as Leslie snugged the rope around her neck
and muzzle. I checked the cow's gum color and eyes,
her skin tension and pulse. She appeared to be well
hydrated, but obviously stressed. I patted her in
sympathy, and went to her rear end to do the manual
exam of her reproductive tract. The rope of tissue
that hung from her vulva turned out to be a calf's tail,
wrapped in a little bit of amniotic sac. It was definitely
a breech calf. Further exploration revealed the calf
to be wedged tightly into the cow's pelvis and already
bloated in death.

I sat back, thinking, then turned to Mr. Duvall, who
sat watching me carefully, his chin resting on his hands,
folded one over the other on his cane. "Well?" he asked
tiredly.

"Breech," I informed him. "And dead. Real dead.
Big calf, too."

"Now you're going to tell me only a C-Section
will save her!" he almost bellowed, startling me into
drawing away from him. "Damn you vets!"

Mrs. Duvall, who had trundled up on her own ATV
4-wheeler earlier, walked over to Mr. Duvall. She laid
a hand on his shoulder. "Now, Arnold," she crooned
soothingly. "Give her a chance to finish." She nodded

at me to continue, a small, grim smile on her face.

"The calf is dead already," I repeated. "We can do a fetotomy; that is, we can dismember the calf and remove it that way. It's a little easier on the cow, and will give her a better chance of survival. Plus, it'll mean she might be salvageable as a breeding animal. But that will depend on the damage to her uterus," I concluded. I watched Mr. Duvall's face change as he contemplated what I'd just said.

"No C-section?" he asked.

"Not at this point," I assured him.

"Do what you can," he said, shaking his head sadly at the cow. "She's going to die anyway."

With that vote of confidence, such as it was, I signaled Leslie to come with me back to my truck, to help me get out my fetotomy equipment.

Fetotomies can be exhausting jobs. First, you must assess the cow's condition to determine if she might be capable of surviving the ordeal. Many things factor into how long the process will take; things like the size of the cow and the size of the fetus, and how tightly the calf is wedged in the birth canal. Other questions needed answers, such as how long the calf had been dead, what position the calf was lying in, how damaged the cow's uterus and vagina might be. You never know, really, until you went to work on it.

This particular calf had been dead a while, probably for 24 hours or so. Once a calf dies in utero, the body heat of the cow accelerates its decomposition. Normally a very warm 102 degrees F, a cow's core body temperature rises with fever, stress and illness. This is good and this is bad. It's bad, because the toxins of the decomposing calf poison the cow. Good, because a rotting carcass is actually easier to dismember and remove than a freshly dead one is.

It is a nauseatingly smelly job, to deliver a dead calf. The highly lubricating fluids of a normal birth process are long gone and the watery substance produced by the disintegrating fetus is not slippery in the least. It clings to every piece of fabric it can touch, it seeps into the pores of your skin, and its odor lingers for days afterward. It's an odor you, as a veterinarian, tend to acknowledge and ignore. Ignore, that is, until days later when you notice bystanders wrinkling their noses in disgust at your presence. Then you rush home and scrub for the hundredth time with every cleaning product in the bathroom and under the kitchen sink. It's a smell you end up waiting to disappear as your body replaces your death-smell-impregnated epidermal cells with fresh, clean skin cells. It's a smell that never really leaves your aura until calving season has been over by a couple of weeks.

Leslie stood back as far as she could from the cow, ready with equipment, ready to assist, but not before absolutely necessary. She cupped one hand over her mouth and nose as she handed me what I needed. I couldn't blame her at all. I had to kneel behind the sick cow, my nose within a few inches of her rump as I navigated the crowded birth canal, looking for a way to begin the job of removing the calf from its exhausted momma.

Both of the rear legs of the calf were bent completely forward in the cow, the toes far out of reach inside the womb. Even with lots of lubricating gel it was still difficult to work my hand down to one of the hocks. The cow, tired from her two days of labor, offered only token strains. An epidural was not going to be necessary to work on her.

My first cut was going to be an attempt to remove a rear leg at the hip. It was very important to make a clean cut through the hip to minimize the amount of sharp bone fragments that would be a risk to the delicate lining of the cow's uterus. I would have to first thread a long piece of cutting wire over the front of the calf's thigh and then between the buttocks of the calf. The wire must be positioned as high into the leg, as close to the hip as possible to optimize the removal of that leg.

After a good bit of time spent grunting and sweating and pushing, adding lubricant often, I was able to get the wire where I needed it to be. Leslie helped me thread the fetotome, the part of the tool that would prevent the saw wire from cutting the cow. She positioned herself to begin the sawing action.

With a "ripe" calf, such as this one was, that first cut often released a gush of fluid from the body of the calf, as well as a large volume of gas, the odor of which was usually ten times more powerful than what was already in the air. I held my breath as Leslie began the cut, as my job was to remain on the ground behind the cow. I had to keep an arm inserted in the cow, guiding the fetotome with my hand and holding it in position. For this I went to school for four years? Yes, I did. On any of these gruesome cases, I could do the work as long as I kept reminding myself that it was a life-saving procedure for the animal.

I glanced at Mr. Duvall. He sat unmoving on his ATV, his hands still folded over the top of his cane, his chin resting fitfully on them. Mrs. Duvall had gotten into the seat of the ATV beside him and they watched the proceedings worriedly.

Leslie worked the saw rapidly and skillfully and within a couple of minutes, the serrated wire had sliced through the skin and rotting muscle of the calf's thigh, into the soft bone, and out the rear of the dead calf. With a little juggling, the severed leg was removed from the cow.

The leg was huge with bloat, heavy with fluid. I dragged it a distance from the cow, hoping to lessen the smell and the numbers of flies that had found us. Flies settled greedily on the calf's leg, and I returned to the cow. She had acquired a little life, it seemed.

Apparently, removing the massive limb had reduced a good deal of pressure on her pelvic nerves. She shifted her weight forward as if to rise, decided against it, and eased back. She grunted as she strained in labor. The rear end of the calf bulged from her vagina, the extra room made by the removal of the swollen leg allowing the calf's body some freedom to move outward about six inches. The cow strained again, and a gush of foul liquid flowed to the ground. I waited to see what the cow would do next. She settled down onto her brisket again, that far-away look returning to her eyes.

I re-examined her. Without that one leg, the delivery was beginning to look like a possibility. It was pretty nasty behind that cow. As I knelt in the brew of mud and rotting uterine tissue and fluid, I asked

Leslie for a new piece of wire, and went to the task of threading it around the remaining hind limb.

The second leg was cut as cleanly as the first and I removed it from the area, leaving it next to its mate to be covered with the increasing number of flies. I batted at a few of the flies that were attracted to the cow. Thank God it was a cool spring day. If it had been as hot as Texas can get early in the year, this job would have been a lot worse. As it was, the job was going a lot more smoothly than I had anticipated. I confidently knelt behind the cow again, signaling to Leslie to hand me a long calving chain. I would loop the chain around the pelvis, in order to be able to ease the rest of the calf's body out of the cow with the calf puller.

As I positioned the chain, Leslie trotted to the truck for the calf puller. The calf puller, also called a calf jack, is a long metal pole with a ratcheting mechanism, a come-along, at one end. A U-shaped piece of hardware, known as a butt plate, was mounted on the other end. The butt plate fitted below the cow's rear hip bones, on the back of her rear legs. A strap passed over the hips to keep the butt plate from slipping down to her hocks. My calf puller was designed with a spiraling bar as the pole attached to the butt plate. The come-along, attached to the body of the calf with a chain, would travel away from the cow as the operator worked the handle. The calf would be slowly ratcheted from the cow. How much tension was applied during this process was important. Too much, and the cow would be injured or the calf pulled apart before it was removed from the cow. To do it right took a little finesse and a little skill, mixed with a little bit of luck and a little bit of prayer.

Another problem that could occur if the delivery was too fast was a complete prolapse of the uterus from the cow. Never pretty, always life-threatening, a prolapse was a mostly preventable and mostly correctable problem of any calf delivery.

We placed the equipment carefully in position. Leslie would handle the ratchet and I would guide the calf up and over the pelvis. It was somewhat difficult to remove the rest of this calf. Besides being bloated and large, the calf's hair and ribs were lying in the opposite direction of the pull. It was dry, too, and we had to stop often to apply lubricant. Finally, though, the carcass popped free of the cow. A large volume of foul, bloody liquid flowed from the cow, followed by fragments and sections of the rotting afterbirth. The calf delivery looked like a success.

Mr. Duvall pounded his cane hard onto the ground behind me. "You did it!" he exclaimed. "You got it out of her without a C-section!" Mrs. Duvall clapped her hands together once, and grinned happily at me. I stood up, tired, filthy, smelling like the calf, and grinned back.

"Now we have to clean up the cow, and see if she can stand up," I said. Leslie had dragged the calf puller, still attached to the remains of the calf, to one side and removed the chains. I went to help her haul the equipment to the pickup, where we would clean it up before stowing it in its compartment in the truck bed.

The cow was actually looking brighter. She belched loudly, and cast her eyes back toward the humans behind her. She wrinkled her nose at the smell of her calf, extending her neck toward it. She snuffled. Satisfied that the calf was dead, she settled back on her chest, making no attempt to stand up.

Leslie and I gathered the supplies we'd need to flush the cow's uterus of the disintegrating placenta, the antibiotic uterine boluses that would be placed in the womb, as well as an injection of antibiotic and a calcium/magnesium IV to help her recover more quickly from the ordeal. We did our work quickly and efficiently, and then stepped back from the cow. The moment of truth had come. I shushed at the cow, flapping my hand towel at her head, encouraging her to stand. She ignored me.

"Use this," Mr. Duvall suggested, passing the long cattle prod to me. I took it, and before applying it anywhere on the cow, I pressed the on button to test it for power. It buzzed menacingly. The cow heard it, and was immediately motivated to action. She sucked in a quick breath and lunged forward, hoping to escape the sting of the hot shot. I didn't even need to touch her with it, the buzz of the cattle prod alone enough to cause her to attempt to stand up.

She didn't gain her feet on that first attempt, but she gave it a powerful try. She got almost up, but the weakness in her rear end from two days of a calf pressing on her pelvic nerves and two days of labor refused to let her stand up all the way. She sank back to her chest, her eyes now full of worry over the cattle prod that had buzzed the warning to her. I set the appliance to one side.

"She'll be able to get up in awhile," I told the Duvalls. "Let her rest. She's had a hard two days."

Leslie and I retired to the truck to clean the calving equipment and put it away.

The cow did stand up, but it took her three days to recover enough to do so. The Duvalls diligently brought her water and food during that time, urging her to get up, so the circulation in her legs would not be compromised. She was wobbly a long time afterward, but did remain on the Diamond D Ranch. Within six months of her tragic delivery, she conceived again. Her second calf was born normal and healthy nine months later. I saw that cow almost every time I returned to the Duvalls, but only as she grazed in the pasture with her herd mates. She never had another experience like her first calving again, and was a good, productive cow for years afterward.

The Duvalls were delighted with my work that day. Over the ensuing years I did many other veterinary jobs for them, all of them successful. As a matter of fact, I considered the Diamond D as my "charmed" ranch—everything I did for them, regardless of how ominous the call sounded when they rang up the clinic for me to come, turned out well.

✳

I decided it was that long drive to their place that did it. It allowed me a lot of time to pray for help and to consider treatment options for the case I would be tending. I had time to forget the worries of the clinic and concentrate on what I would be doing next. And it allowed time for a gathering of the forces whose job it was to keep me safe and assist me in my work.

Chapter Ten

A Grandmother and Her Grandson

God made all the creatures and gave them our love and our fear, to give sign, we and they are His children, one family here. ~Robert Browning

Once in practice for myself, I answered just about any call for help that I could. I tended to treat the people and the animals equally, regardless of the owner's financial situation or the pedigree tacked on the animal. Many of my cattle clients had only small herds of cattle. Often, they were retired folks trying their hands at long-held dreams of being ranchers.

Those people tended to know little about cows and it made for interesting work. My favorites, though were the older folks who had lived their entire lives on family homesteads, keeping a few head of cattle for extra income, or for milk and meat. Some of the most interesting calls I went out on as a veterinarian tending to cattle came from elderly country folks seeking veterinary help for their animals.

One afternoon my receptionist, Leslie, answered a phone call from a Ruthie Washington. The caller had the trembling voice of an old black woman. She had a cow needing help; she said it was having trouble "finding" its calf. I was a little confused as to why the lady was calling me about a lost calf, and asked her to explain what she meant.

"She's been trying to find her calf since this morning," Ms. Washington repeated. "She's been trying real hard, too. I need someone to come help her. It's her first calf."

While I puzzled for a minute over why a veterinarian might be necessary to help find a missing calf, Ms. Washington added another clue to her message. "There's one little foot showing," she said softly. "All that pushing, and that's all that cow can find."

Ah! I suddenly understood what the lady was telling me. Her cow was in labor and had not been able to produce the calf. One foot was all that showed for all the cow's efforts, and the owner was worried. I had just been educated on a quaint expression the more respectful older people used to refer to labor in a cow. "Finding her calf" was a polite way to say the cow was in labor.

Ms. Washington was right to be worried; cows as well as their calves can die from dystocia, the medical word for a difficult delivery. Now that I understood her problem, I agreed to come to her assistance, if the cow was penned. Mrs. Washington assured me that the cow was caught up in a lot. She had a grandson, too, who would be there to lend assistance, if needed. She gave me directions to her place in a breathy voice that sounded like it was the most use she'd given her vocal cords in awhile. By the time she finished giving me the twists and turns of the various roads I would be traveling, she sounded exhausted. I was happy she had a grandson to help out. I checked my pickup for the needed supplies and equipment, and headed out into the country.

Ruthie Washington was just as old as her voice suggested, if not older. She was waiting patiently on her front porch when I pulled up, a frail-looking, dusky black woman with thin white hair. She wore a mid-length lightweight cotton frock and a worn sunbonnet, a common enough attire for the elderly women I worked for over the years in Houston County. She stood up cautiously, using a walking cane made from a gnarled oak branch to help her. We introduced ourselves to each other, and she expressed her gratitude for my willingness to help her. "Call me Miz Ruthie," she suggested. Her grandson had not arrived to help yet, and she was apologetic and agitated about that.

"Where is the cow?" I asked, thinking if it was in the pen, I could get to work with or without the grandson to help.

"She's in the lot behind the house," Miz Ruthie answered, waving with her cane in the general direction of the lot. "We can go on down there now, if you please."

"I'd like to see the cow as soon as possible," I said, "so I can know what I'll need to get from my truck to help her." Miz Ruthie nodded in understanding, and carefully started easing down the porch steps, holding tight to the rail. She did not talk much, putting her strength into making the slow trek to the barn lot behind the house. I walked in pace with her, on guard to offer a supporting hand if she needed it.

I had a special place in my heart for the elderly country folk of Houston County, who tried hard to hold onto their independence, their way of life, and their little plots of land. Often, with no one to help them, their facilities fell into disrepair. You never knew what you were going to find on this type of backwoods establishment. More often than not, the pens were in poor condition with weak fencing, with what seemed just pure luck keeping the animal confined. Sometimes you got a surprise with a well-maintained pen as your workspace.

In this case the pen the owner promised the cow would be restricted to was not exactly a pen. It was more a small pasture at least four acres in size, surrounded by ratty, rusting barbwire. Miz Ruthie's heifer, a smallish Hereford crossbred type, was pacing the fence, worrying for her herd-mates which grazed out of sight in the larger pasture. The cow had a distinct wobble in her stride, no doubt from the pressure of the calf on her pelvic nerves. This I considered a factor in my favor. Veterinary school had not taught me how to throw a rope, and no amount of desire would make a cowhand out of a lariat-challenged person. Anything that would slow a cow down and make a rope catch more likely was a good thing.

There was a lean-to shed in one corner of the large lot, surrounded by an interesting-looking fence. On closer inspection, the shed's fence was revealed to be old, rusty bedsprings, stripped of their fabric and padding, tied end to end with baling wire to form a barrier of sorts. I had my doubts the fence could hold the cow, especially when there was a stranger in green coveralls chasing her while wildly slinging a rope. I wondered where the grandson was. As if reading my thoughts, Miz Ruthie glanced back toward her house and said, "Michael should be along any time now." We both turned and looked toward the house hopefully. No one was there, no sound of an engine drifted up the road to the house. We studied the road silently, willing the young man to appear. I sighed.

"Miz Ruthie, I'm going to bring my truck around, park it near that lean-to," I said. "Then I'll see if I can't walk that cow up to the pen." She nodded, and slowed-stepped her way toward the shade of the shed.

I hurried back toward my pickup and got in. Before cranking the engine, I hopefully searched the road for the grandson. No tale-tell motor hum of an approaching vehicle, no cloud of dust announcing his imminent arrival. I fired up my truck, put it in gear, and trundled it over to the pen.

When I cut off the rumbling diesel engine, I could hear a soft crooning drifting over the pasture. Miz

Ruthie stood by a gate—more correctly an opening in the bed-spring pen, holding a feed bucket with one hand while supporting herself with the cane in her other hand. She was calling to the heifer, who stood facing the lean-to, ears pitched forward toward Miz Ruthie. I did not get out of my truck, but sat there, waiting to see if the little cow would respond by going to her mistress. I watched as the cow's back end swayed gently side to side. She stopped once to hump up against a contraction. When the contraction ended, she lowed to Miz Ruthie, and continued to waddle across the pasture toward the pen. I stayed where I was, unwilling to do anything that might cause the cow to bolt away from the lean-to. Miz Ruthie continued to coo softly to the approaching cow.

Behind me, I heard the sound of humming motor. I turned to see a small-sized pickup flying up the dirt road to the house, a huge cloud of red dust kicked up by its wheels hanging in the air behind it. What bad timing, I thought. Just as the cow gets to the pen, here comes someone to scare her away.

Luckily, I was wrong. Apparently, the pickup was a known quantity to the heifer. She did not slow down her swaying pace toward the pen, and in a minute or so had slid through the opening and walked up to Miz Ruthie to accept a range cube from the bucket the old lady held.

A handsome young black man emerged from the newly arrived pickup. He was dressed in a clean T-shirt with a logo for a local gym on the front, blue jeans, high-topped sports sneakers, and a black do-rag tightened down over his close-cropped hair. This must be Michael, I thought. For a moment he stood unsmiling, assessing the situation in front of him. He solemnly nodded to me, then hustled toward the old woman in the pen. He quickly and quietly slid behind the cow and blocked the opening back into the pasture with one of the old bedsprings leaning against the fence. The cow was now in a pen about 30 feet square with a small lean-to in one corner.

I got out of my truck. Instantly, the heifer jerked her head up and stopped chewing on the range cubes, turning slightly to eye me suspiciously. She turned away, heading for the now-closed gap. A moment of truth. Would she attempt to jump or push her way out? She did not. She stopped, blew loudly out her nose, and shook her head. Miz Ruthie had started her slow, stately walk back toward the gate that opened into her house's back yard. The young man hurried across the lot, meeting us at the gate.

"This here's Michael, my grandson," Miz Ruth informed me. "Michael helps me with the cows sometimes. He ain't never been here to help with a birthin'." She glanced at Michael. "You got to help the doctor," she told him. "Do like she tells you, mind you."

"Yes, Gramma," Michael replied, nodding respectfully toward his grandmother. He and I looked each other up and down, wondering which of us was going to help the other.

"We need to tie up the cow," I said to Michael. "Can you rope?"

Michael pursed his lips, looked down, and made a mark in the dust with the toe of his sneaker. "No ma'am," he answered. "Never could."

"Me neither," I acknowledged sadly. "But let's see what we can do."

I passed my rope from my left to my right hand. Even though I am left-handed, most ropes, because of the way the fibers are twisted in the construction of the rope, are made to be thrown right-handed. I figured that was part of the reason I was a poor roper. I didn't have a left-handed rope, so I had to throw right-handed. I was not very good at it. Nonetheless, some days I got lucky and the rope went where I wanted it to when I threw it.

That day was such a day. The heifer, concentrating on a contraction, was standing humped up and motionless; her tail half- raised, eyes unfocused, her jaws stopped mid-motion in a chew on a range cube. She wasn't that far away from me. I had a chance of catching her. I shook out a length of the rope, gripped it firmly, gave it a half-twirl over my head and sent it sailing toward the cow. It settled over her horns neatly. Almost in surprise, I jerked the slack and tightened the rope snuggly. I had caught the cow, and made it look like I knew what I was doing. If Miz Ruthie or Michael were surprised or impressed, they didn't show it.

The next trick was to find a post stout enough to secure the rope to. The cow was actually cooperating nicely, as if she knew that help was on the way. A suitable post appeared to be one of the lean-to's support posts. I moved toward the cow's hip, shushing at her, asking her to move toward the post. She did so in a calm manner, allowing me time to wrap a loop of the rope around the post. With the rope snugged down around her horns, a halter around her head would not be necessary. She stood still as another contraction took hold of her attention. I scooted out of the pen to my truck for supplies.

Michael followed me over and helped pick up and carry some of the equipment. His eyes got a little big as I assembled the calf puller I would probably be using. I put the chains in a bucket. Michael gulped slowly. I got the OB sleeves, a gallon water and the OB lube, and we carried it all into the pen to the cow.

My first tentative exploration of the cow's inner pelvis, though gentle, was enough to cause her to fall, stiff-legged, over on her side and begin to strain fiercely against the pressure. Michael jumped to one side, alarmed. He had looked stunned when I had passed my gloved arms into the cow, searching for the reason the calf could not emerge from its mother. It now probably looked like I had killed the cow. It was obvious he had never before witnessed an assisted calving.

"She alright?" Miz Ruthie called to me.

"Yes ma'am," I answered. "She's fine. She's in pretty heavy labor, though."

The calf's head was right there, positioned between the knees of the calf in the pelvic canal. I put two fingers into the calf's mouth, and got a strong suckle reflex in return.

"The calf's alive," I reported. "We're going to try to get him out in a few minutes."

The calf was in the proper position, just a little tight and a wee bit large. I felt confident that with a little help, the calf could be delivered in short order. I had Michael pass me a chain, which I affixed to one fore leg.

After bringing the other front leg further out, I asked for another chain, which Michael passed over to me quickly. I ran one hand up behind the head of the calf; it felt right. Now for the delivery.

I attached a handle to each of the chains, and gave them to Michael. He looked at them speechlessly.

"When I say pull, pull whichever chain I say to, left or right," I instructed. "Pull steady, no jerking. OK?"

"OK," Michael nodded doubtfully. With his eyes wide, his long fingers closing tightly over the handles, he eased back into a brace, ready to pull.

The heifer moaned and twisted around when traction was applied to the chains, straining to deliver the calf. After a moment's hesitation, the calf's fore legs emerged, one slightly in front of the other. Just the tip of its nose emerged also. The nostrils twitched. That was as far as it got, with Michael leaning back and pulling for all he was worth. I joined him, but the calf didn't budge. It was time to get the mechanical calf puller.

I sent Michael over to get the puller from where it leaned against the fence. He was puzzled about it, and watched silently as I placed it in the proper position against the cow's butt. I hooked up the chains, and indicated to Michael to step up to handle the calf puller.

"I'm going to guide the calf's head out," I told him. "I want you to work the lever on this puller when I say, and stop when I say, alright?" He nodded gravely.

With the cow lying on the ground like she was, it meant that I had to kneel down behind her to work with her. I passed my right hand into the cow, and cupped my fingers behind the calf's ears. With my say-so, Michael began a slow ratcheting of the puller, coupled with a downward push on the long bar. With my hand behind guiding it, the calf's head popped free of the cow. With a little extra traction, the calf's body began to slide out easily. The calf's eyes sprang open, his mouth opened, and a watery bawl sounded. A second later, the entire calf was on the ground, wiggling and wet. The cow heaved, and a gush of amniotic fluid flooded from her. She sat up when the calf bawled a second time, answering it with a bawl of her own.

I dragged the newborn calf a little way away from the cow, removed the chains from its legs, and helped it sit up on its chest. The cow stayed where she was, resting. I cleaned up the calf's nose, satisfied with the outcome of the procedure. With Michael's help, I hauled my equipment back to the truck. We went back to the pen, where Miz Ruthie stood watching the cow and calf from outside the salvaged bedspring fence.

I went to the cow to remove the rope from her horns. After a moment, she heaved to her feet, stood a moment swaying, then turned and went to her calf. I joined Miz Ruthie and Michael, and we watched the cow snuffle over her calf and sing to it as it attempted to rise to its feet.

"Well, Grandson," Miz Ruthie said to the young man standing next to her, her hands crossed and resting on the top of her cane. "What do you think of that?"

The youth shook his head solemnly. "I know if I was that cow," he stated solemnly, "I'd stay as far away from a bull as I could from here on."

The old woman stamped the ground fiercely with her cane, twisted around to face her grandson, and looked him in the eye. She poked him firmly with her index finger in the center of his chest. Nose to nose with him, from between clenched teeth she hissed at him, "And you *remember* that next time you go to take a young girl out on a date!"

❋

The work was interesting, but the people made it memorable.

CHAPTER ELEVEN

ANOTHER GRANDMOTHER AND HER GRANDSONS

I could not have slept tonight if I'd left that helpless creature to perish. ~Abraham Lincoln, in response to friends who chided him for delaying them when he stopped to pick up a fallen bird.

Actually, many of my clients were elderly. A number of them had been born and raised in Houston County, a few right there on the very land they still ranched. The cows they fed were usually only a few in number. The cows often had pet names and were spoken of fondly by their owners. I am sure the lives these people lived, going out daily to tend to the needs of their small herds, contributed to their longevity. Over the years I did large animal medicine, I was to meet and work for many senior citizens who lived full lives on small farms and ranches across the county. They were, truly, my favorite type of client. They were mostly all honest, hardworking individuals who expected nothing less from others. Their sense of decency was strong, as well their pride in their independence.

I broke my left foot in the late spring in 1991. The four bones of the instep were crushed in a freaky incident on my own home property, broken by one of my own horses. It wasn't the horse's fault, and it might not even have been my fault. At any rate, I ended up with a plaster cast on my leg that reached from the toes to the knee.

While it was inconvenient to be crippled while practicing small animal medicine, doing large animal medicine while sporting a six-pound plaster cast on one leg made for difficult work. The cast was not only heavy but itchy, too. It was bad enough having to wear it when I hobbled down to my home barn to take care of my own horses and other animals. I couldn't picture myself clunking around on the cast in field conditions, doing cattle or horse work for others. I decided to suspend any cattle or horse work, in the field or at the clinic, until the cast was removed in eight weeks.

Most of my cattle and horse clients were very understanding. Those needing routine care for their animals were willing to reschedule until after my bones had mended. Emergency calls were referred to one of the other veterinary clinics in town.

Much as I regretted having to refer my clients elsewhere for their emergency veterinary needs, I must admit I was not unhappy. After all, it was summer. While winter weather can make fieldwork miserable, the heat of the Texas summers made it pure hell. Temperatures over the 100-degree range were not uncommon even in early June. The humidity of the region often increased the heat index to nearly unbearable heights. Add in the accentuation of smells by the heat, the hoards of flies and mosquitoes at the height of their breeding season, and no, I wasn't missing the field calls that summer much at all.

As it is, though, one never knows what's going to happen day-to-day in veterinary medicine. I'd had the cast encasing my leg for seven weeks. One more week and I'd be free of that plaster torture device. One more week and I could throw away the coat hanger wire I used to get at the itchy spots under the cast. One more week and I could wash the sweat and used-up skin cells from my leg. One more week and I could shave my leg again. Ahh.

Things were quiet for me in the large animal department, as news of my injury apparently had circulated in the community. When the clinic phone rang one early July morning, I was not expecting a cow owner to be calling. My receptionist, Leslie, answered the phone. After a couple minutes exchanging some information with the caller, she hung up the phone and turned to me to tell me what the call was about. The caller, she said, sounded like an elderly black woman. Her name was Hattie McCloud, and she had never used our services before. She said she had a cow in labor, and it didn't look like the cow would be able to have the calf without help. Leslie had tried to explain the situation with my broken foot and the cast to Mrs. McCloud. She had suggested the woman call one of the other veterinarians in town for assistance, and had given her the numbers of their clinics. Mrs. McCloud had thanked Leslie, and hung up.

About fifteen minutes later, the phone rang again, and again the caller was Hattie McCloud. She had called the other veterinarians in the area, she said, but not one of them was available to help her. As a matter of fact, she had been told by each of the other clinics' receptionists that the veterinarian was out of town for the Fourth of July holiday. She had called my clinic again, wanting to know if there was any way that I could help her.

Leslie offered the phone to me. She thought that I might be able to convince the woman of my injury's hindrance on my ability to work, since she had been unable to get the message across to Mrs. McCloud. I took the phone receiver from her.

"Mrs. McCloud?" I inquired, while running a hanger wire down the inside of my cast. "Did you understand what Leslie told you? Did she tell you why I cannot come out to help you?"

"Yes, she did," responded Mrs. McCloud, in a soft, gentle voice. "And I understand about your broken foot. But I need some help out here with my cow. I have four grandsons here to help you, if you'll only come. Or if you tell one of them what to do, maybe they can help my cow."

I shook my head at Leslie, who was watching me out the corner of her eye. "Mrs. McCloud, that probably isn't a good idea. A trained veterinarian or someone else with experience needs to be there to pull that calf. There's no one to help you?"

"No one but my grandsons, and they don't know what to do," Mrs. McCloud replied in a mournful whisper. "This is a good cow. She'll die if she don't get that calf out. I'm sure my grandsons can help, though. They are good boys, nice and strong, too. They's already here. Could you please come on out?"

I was a sucker for a sob story in those days, especially from the elderly. I'm still that way, I guess. I didn't know how to respond to this desperate lady. I couldn't think of anyone that I knew who might be able to help her out. I chewed on my lower lip, wondering what to do.

"Doctor?" came the soft, smoky old voice. "Will you come?"

I stood up from my desk. "Give me directions out to your place, Mrs. McCloud," I said. "And make sure that cow is in a pen or has a rope on her before I get there."

The gratitude was evident in the woman's voice as she gave me precise directions to her farm. I wrote them down, told her I'd be there as soon as possible, and hung up the phone.

"I can't believe you're going out there," Leslie stated, shaking her head in disbelief.

"Well, what else can I do?" I said. "No one else is around to go. I can't just let the cow die."

"What about your cast?" Leslie asked, hands on hips.

"I'll take some plastic bags, wrap it up so it won't get dirty," I answered. "It's coming off in a week anyway. It's probably already healed up."

"Well, don't get stepped on again," she replied grimly, as I hobbled away to prepare for the run to the country.

It was close to noon and hot outside. The blast of

humid air as I stepped out the door of the clinic nearly sent me reeling. What the heck was I thinking? I checked the contents of my truck, and then went back in the clinic to change into my cow clothes.

Normally for call outs, I wore a coverall over my jeans and T-shirt, one of those short-sleeved jumpsuits that covered a person neck to ankle. I knew the work ahead would be grueling in this steamy hot weather. I hoped the cow was tied under a nice, big shade tree. I hoped Mrs. McCloud had a pitcher of iced tea at the ready for my refreshment. I hoped the calf was situated so that a flick of my wrist would straighten the malposition, and I would be out of there—clean, dry and my cast intact. I always hoped for the best in an upcoming and unknown situation.

I tended to develop heat stress symptoms rather easily when the heat index was high, as it was that day. I decided to wear just the coverall with no jeans or T-shirt underneath, to try to keep a little cooler. I put an old sneaker on my right foot, and was ready to go.

Hattie McCloud lived in a little family community about ten miles out of town. She was obviously the matriarch of the extended family who lived in a collection of mobile homes and small frame houses on the farm. The land had been homesteaded probably a century earlier. There were a number of such communities in Houston County. I liked going out to them. There was something enviable about having members of your family—your parents, your brothers and sisters, your cousins, aunts and uncles—living nearby to help out in your daily life.

I found the row of mailboxes that marked the entrance to the McCloud property. A young black man waited in the shade of a large pecan tree near the gate. He quickly opened the gate when he understood I was the one he waited for. He indicated a house just up the lane as my destination.

Mrs. McCloud's home was a rambling old frame house in need of paint and a couple of braces under the roof of the front porch. A small flower garden in the front yard bloomed with a perfusion of colors, obviously tended to lovingly, weeded and watered through the summer heat. Mrs. McCloud was seated in a metal yard chair on the shady front porch. She stood up as I braked in the driveway. She looked to be at least 90 years old. She was tiny, bent from age and the trials of her life. She wore a thin cotton dress that reached to midcalf. An old-fashioned sunbonnet shielded her thinly-haired gray head from the heat of the sun. Looking out of place on the old woman in her dated clothing was a pair of brand new, sparkling white canvas running shoes, laced over crew socks that went half way up the lady's thin old dusky black legs. Moving carefully, leaning on her cane and the banister rail of the steps to the porch, she came down the steps to greet me.

The young man who had opened the gate for me strode up. From inside the house came another young black man, tall, serious-looking.

"Mrs. McCloud, I'm Dr. Cooper-Chase," I introduced myself after I had hobbled around to the front of the truck.

She nodded, barely touching my extended hand. "Hattie," she said. "Folks just call me Miz Hattie. These are my grandsons, Will and John. They'll take you down to the cow." She looked down at my cast-enclosed leg. "I am so sorry about your injury, and I can't thank you enough for coming out here," she said, ever so softly. "No one else would come."

"I'm glad I could come to help," I replied sincerely. "I'll come back to you here on the porch when we're finished with the cow, let you know what we found."

Not one to expend energy unnecessarily talking on a hot Texas day, Miz Hattie nodded. She indicated with her cane to the young men to go with me. Will, the taller of the two men, stepped up to me.

"The cow's in the pasture behind the house," he informed me. "We got a rope on her, but she can't get up. Just follow me around in your truck."

"Do you want a ride?" I asked them.

"No ma'am" they both answered in unison. "It ain't far," John said. "We'll walk." They turned and started around the house in long strides. I got back in the truck to follow.

Just behind the house was a small field. Will held the gate open for me to drive through. About a hundred feet inside the fence lay a large tawny brown dairy-type cow, propped up on her chest. She was in obvious distress. Between her attempts to deliver her calf and the heat, she was showing signs of exhaustion. She panted, open-mouthed, stopping when necessary to grunt against a contraction.

Two more young black men, teenagers, stood beside her. They had thoughtfully provided the cow with a bucket of water and a small flake of hay, for which she had no interest in her present condition. And unfortunately, she was lying out in the direct noonday sun. The nearest shade tree was at least another fifty feet away.

I stopped my pickup within fifteen feet of where the cow lay. She paid me no heed. I got out and did a quick assessment of her over-all condition. The grass in the field was short, dry, and brittle, and crackled as I humped my cast-enclosed leg over it. The ground itself was hard and dry. It radiated the sun's heat back, and the air shimmered with the humidity. Sweat was gleaming on the brows of all the young men around the cow, and their shirts were beginning to dampen. I could feel rivulets of perspiration running down my sides already. With a hand towel I wiped my brow and upper lip free of sweat. A heat-induced headache was sure to develop before long, I knew. I had to get to work.

With assistance from John, I got my water jugs, soap and gloves from my truck. I carefully positioned my wounded leg behind me as I knelt by the cow. After a quick vaginal examination of the cow, I stood up again. The calf was presented with the front legs folded at the knees. I'd have to correct their position before the cow could deliver. I hobbled back to my truck for the chains and handles, explaining to the young men what my intentions were.

First, though, I took a plastic trash bag and a roll of duct tape I had brought along for the purpose, and wrapped my cast protectively in the bag, taping it firmly in place. I pulled my bandanna out of my hip pocket and tied it over my head.

They were a quiet grouping of young men. Serious, unsmiling faces listened to me explain what I wanted each of them to do. Once I had corrected the calf's legs' position, I would place a chain on each leg. John and Will would each have an OB handle to attach to a chain. Theodore, one of the teenagers, would stand at the ready with the OB lube, to replenish the lube on my gloved hands as necessary. Darius, the other teenager, would stay with the cow's head, directing her should she try to rise and leave. Each nodded solemnly in understanding to what I asked each to do.

I sure wished we were under one of those tall, shady trees. I looked wistfully over to one whose leaves fluttered in a gentle breeze passing through them. I looked away from the cool shade, took a deep breath, and knelt down again, gloved, behind the cow.

It was hot work. The calf was alive, and resisted my intervention in her life. Twice I'd have a small hoof in my hand, and would be working it carefully up over the pelvis when the calf would wrest it away, back into the depths of the uterus. When I finally got one foot in the proper position, the cow strained mightily, and caused the calf's head to emerge from the uterus and into the birth canal. Still, with one bent leg, it wasn't going to be able to come out. I had to hold the calf back each time the cow strained, to prevent the calf from further wedging in the birth canal, then go back to work trying to position the other front leg.

Sweat was pouring off me. I could hardly see for the salty fluid flowing into my eyes. I couldn't wipe my eyes either, not with messy plastic gloves on my hands and arms. Flies, attracted by the cow's blood and vaginal fluid, buzzed around and landed on my face. I could not swipe at them. I had to keep working. At one point, my good leg braced against the ground as I pushed to hold the calf against the straining cow, I glanced around me. Each of the young men was waiting to help, silent, tensed, so solemn in appearance

I almost chuckled. Behind us, coming from the house through the small back yard, was Hattie McCloud. She carried an umbrella, red and white striped, over her head, while leaning on her cane. Her gleaming white sneakers flashed in the sun. She carefully opened the gate, crossed into the field, shut the gate, and turned to move cautiously toward us.

I was still kneeling on the ground behind the cow, working to free the calf's other leg as I watched the old lady walking carefully across the field, that bright umbrella shading her, those shoes reflecting the sun's rays into my eyes. The calf's foot I wrestled with moved just enough, and I got it; it suddenly slid into position. I drew it out into the light of day and I quickly looped a chain above the fetlock, and handed the end of each chain to Will and John.

"Okay," I said to the two young men, who waited with serious expressions for my orders, "When I say, pull slow and steady. Don't jerk on the chain, just pull slow and steady unless I say otherwise."

Each young man nodded in understanding of my instructions.

I put one hand back into the cow and found the calf's chin. I guided it to sit between the front legs.

"Slow and easy," I instructed.

Slowly, carefully, they pulled on the calf's front legs, first John, then Will, as I indicated. The calf's nose popped into the hot air and the nostrils wrinkled. The cow gave a heave, and the calf slid out, easily, onto the ground. Will and John dragged the calf, a light brown-colored heifer, a few feet from the cow.

The young men began to smile and laugh with relief as they slapped each other on the back, all the while admiring the newborn calf. I cautioned Darius not to leave his post by the cow's head, as now was the time she would be most inclined to get up. But the cow ignored her calf. She merely panted in the heat, and made no attempt to get up.

By this time, Miz Hattie had made her slow way over to where her grandsons were removing the OB chains from the calf. She held her umbrella out and over the calf, to shade it from the sun's intense rays.

I got up from my knees. My plaster-encased leg felt like it weighed a hundred pounds. Moisture had fogged the plastic, and my sweat had puddled inside the bag. I tore at the tape, removed the plastic bag. The plaster cast felt soggy from the soaking it had gotten from my perspiration. My coveralls were drenched in sweat. I was drenched, my scalp prickling from the heat. Wow. The heat-induced headache that had knocked at the back of my eyes earlier was now kicking in the door.

Miz Hattie was smiling slightly, nudging the wiggling calf with the tip of her cane. The four young men were standing in a semi-circle, laughing lightly and exclaiming at the sight, pleased to have participated in the event. I wondered if any of them realized I was still there.

I tiredly bent to pick up equipment I had used in the calf delivery to take it to the truck. I got some medicine for the cow, and hobbled around her to give her an injection in the neck. She bawled low, and attempted to get up. I backed away to give her the room she needed. Awkwardly, the cow staggered up on all fours, trailing the pink membrane of afterbirth behind her. She did not seek her calf, merely stood, head extended, panting in the heat.

"Put the calf where she can see it," I suggested, coming around to stand next to Miz Hattie. The two teenagers hefted the calf, and carried it carefully to the front of the cow.

The cow suddenly stopped her panting, snuffling in the direction of the calf. A look of comprehension came to her eyes, and she emitted a low hum, a gentle, quiet noise I loved to hear a mamma cow sing. She reached out with her long tongue, and tasted the little heifer. She began to sing in earnest, washing the calf tenderly with long swipes of her rough tongue. It was pretty to see.

My headache receded a little bit. I stood there watching the cow and calf with Miz Hattie, her four young grandsons strung out in a line beside her.

Suddenly, unexpectedly, and with a lot more energy than I expected from an ancient black woman, Hattie McCloud screeched piercingly. She raised her arms and began to beat her grandsons with her umbrella in one hand and her cane in the other. I was speechless, aghast, watching her flail at those four young men. They were jumping back from her, looks of utter confusion on their faces. They put up their arms to shield their heads from her onslaught, voices raised in objection to her treatment of them. "No, Gramma!" "What did I do?" "Ow ow!"

What the hell was going on?

Her screeching began to sound like words to me. I made out, "Don't you look at her! Don't you dare look at that woman!"

What? What the heck was she telling them? They had not been looking at me; they had been watching the cow and calf! I looked down at myself, wondering what it was she didn't want them to see.

I was soaking wet. My coveralls, a light gray when dry, were dark with sweat. They clung to my skin. They had soaked up my sweat and were now wet and plastered to me. Everywhere except in two places. Stark outlines of my bra and panties stood out in light gray relief against the dark of the sweat-soaked coveralls. My underwear had prevented the cloth of the coveralls over them from getting soaked, too. I was standing there with my underwear outlined.

I quickly plucked at the coveralls, releasing the fabric from my skin, shaking them loose. Miz Hattie had stopped assailing her grandsons, and was huffing and blowing for breath.

"Miz Hattie, it's alright," I assured her, attempting to mollify her by gently patting her bony shoulder. "They didn't see anything. They didn't even look at me. They didn't do anything wrong."

The old lady patted her brow with a handkerchief she had produced from one sleeve of her dress. She glared menacingly at her grandsons as she leaned on her cane. Her umbrella lay half-open and broken on the ground. The four young men had retreated beyond her reach, trying to make themselves look as small as possible. Each was making a concentrated effort not to look in my direction.

"I ain't gonna have no grandchild of mine gettin' in trouble for looking at a white woman's underwear," Miz Hattie declared. She looked me up and down. "You come out here again, young lady, you best wear some clothes under that suit."

"Yes ma'am," I said, chastised.

I continued to pull the wet fabric away from my skin, trying to make it look baggy, as I went to pick up my equipment.

"Let these young men do dat," Miz Hattie snapped at me. She barked at her grandsons. "Git over here and help this lady with this stuff!"

All four of them jumped at her instructions, and keeping a wide berth of their grandmother, circled around to come over to pick up what equipment had been dropped on the ground.

"And don't none of you dare look at her!" she snapped, waving her cane. Each of young the men ducked his head and averted his eyes as they scurried around.

"Now." Miz Hattie drew herself up as straight as she could. The top of her bonneted head barely reached my shoulder. "How much do I owe you for your work?"

I quoted her a price, and she sent her youngest grandson to the house for her change purse. He galloped off quickly. The other three were at a loss as to what to do now. They waited nervously, eyes down, occasionally throwing a glance at their grandmother. I was embarrassed for them as well as myself.

Darius came loping back with his grandmother's change purse. She carefully counted out the bills and gave me my wages. She signaled to Theodore, who scurried to stand in front of her, awaiting orders.

"Open the gate for this woman," she told him. She waved her cane at the others, which caused them to duck defensively. "You all git that cow and calf in some shade, and get her some cool water, and some range cubes to eat." The four grandsons scattered like leaves before a gale force wind to do their grandmother's bidding.

She turned back to me. Her face, a moment ago tight and angry, was relaxed and smiling gently.

"Thank you for coming out here to help us," she said in a voice once again soft and lilting, maybe now a little bit raw from the shouting she had done. "I won't forget your kindness."

* * *

I knew I wouldn't forget the incident either. I realized as I drove out through the gate, waving to Theodore as I left, that I no longer had a headache pounding on my senses. I drove back to the clinic, cheered and satisfied that I had done the right thing by responding to Mrs. McCloud's desperate plea for help with her cow. I also vowed I would from that day forward always wear shorts and a shirt under my coveralls on calls out on hot, humid summer days.

Chapter Twelve

Mr. Albright's Choking Cow

When a man has pity on all living creatures only then is he noble. ~Buddha (563? - 483? B.C.)

I don't wear a wedding ring, for the simple reason I lost mine one night during a calf delivery. I had forgotten to take it off that evening, driving out to the ranch where a cow labored unproductively. Usually, I would remove my ring and hang it from a hook on the turn signal lever in the cab of the truck, and replace it on my finger once I crawled back into the cab for the return home. That fateful evening, however, I had forgotten to remove it and during the indelicate work of extracting the slippery calf from the cow, the ring, well lubricated by the amniotic fluid and obstetric lube, slid from my finger and vanished into the soil and debris of the ranch lot in which we worked. It was never recovered and later my husband replaced it with another ring. So, not seeing a ring on my finger, many people who didn't know me or didn't know my husband, didn't realize I had a spouse keeping the home fire burning while I was out on a job.

One night, close to midnight, while we were home and hard asleep in our bed, the phone rang. Jack, my husband, awoke to the jangle first. Since the telephone rested on the table next to his side of the bed, he reached out, fumbled a bit, picked up the receiver and muttered a groggy "Hello?" I, also jogged from a very sound sleep, lay still, eyes closed, praying that it was a wrong number.

After a quiet pause of several seconds, Jack repeated his "Hello?" After another couple of seconds, he hung the phone up. "Wrong number, I guess," he informed me. "Whoever it was didn't say a thing. They hung up first."

Fine with me. I had had a busy day and was very tired. I snuggled deeper into the covers. I really didn't want to go out in the night to see a sick or injured animal. I just wanted to sleep.

It was not to be. A couple of minutes later the phone shrilled again, seemingly louder without the muffle of dreams between it and my ears. Jack, jarred awake again, picked up the receiver. "Hello," he stated, this time sounding just a little peeved.

A pause. "Yes, she's here," he replied to an inquiry from the caller. I moaned.

"Who is it?" I asked.

"A Mr. Albright," Jack said. "He asked if Dr.

Cooper-Chase was here."

I took the phone, and grunted a cheerless greeting into it.

"Dr. Cooper-Chase?" a man's voice asked cautiously.

"Yes." I confirmed his suspicions.

"Frank Albright here," he said. "I hate to disturb you when you, uh, have company, but I have a cow in trouble."

Company? I sat up, and turned on the bedside lamp. What did he mean by company? I glanced over at Jack, who lay on his back, shielding his eyes from the sudden, rude glare from the lamp.

"Mr. Albright, don't worry about it," I said. "My husband is used to people calling me late at night. What seems to be the problem with your cow?"

There was silence on the other end of the line.

"Mr. Albright?"

"Your husband? You're married!" came to my ear in a tone of disbelief. "Oh, that's good!" Mr. Albright gave a short, relieved chuckle before getting serious. "My cow is real sick. She can't breathe. Can you come look at her? I think she'll die before morning, if she doesn't get tended tonight."

I knew Mr. Albright, having done some work for him in the past. I knew where his ranch was, the well-kept condition of his pens, and the quality of his cows. I also knew he wouldn't call at such an hour of the night unless he thought he had a serious problem. I told him I would be there as soon as possible. He said he would have his grandson out to help, and some floodlights to illuminate the pens we'd be working in. He thanked me for agreeing to see his cow. I hung up the phone.

"What was that about?" Jack asked, his arm still slung over his eyes.

"Mr. Albright thought you were a "guest," I said. "Now I have to go out and look at one of his cows."

"A guest?" Jack asked, sliding his arm from his eyes to look at me. "Seriously?"

"Seriously. He didn't know I was married," I explained.

"Oh!" Jack hitched himself up onto his elbows. "That was probably him who called the first time. Hung up when he heard a man's voice!"

"Yep," I agreed, pulling on my cow clothes, readying to go examine a dyspneic cow. "Want to come along?"

Jack cast a quick eye at the clock, then flopped back flat, pulling his pillow over his face. "Nope," was his answer. I sighed. I wished I could have done the same.

The ranch wasn't far away. When I got to the ranch, Mr. Albright had the cow in the chute but not caught in the head gate. He had a teenaged boy alongside to help. We greeted each other, and if it hadn't been a black night with only a couple floodlights beaming down onto our patient, I'm sure I would have seen that Mr. Albright's face was a shiny red from his somewhat embarrassing call to me. I wasn't going to mention it and apparently, he decided not to, either.

I climbed up on the rails to look over the fence at the black Angus cow standing in the chute. She looked warily up at me, heaving for breath, great ropes of bubbly saliva flowing over her jaws. Her protruding tongue appeared black in the artificial light. She definitely was having a serious problem getting a breath. To me, she appeared to be choking. I jumped down from the fence close to where Mr. Albright waited.

"She can't breathe right," Mr. Albright said worriedly, peering through the rails at his cow. "She was fine this afternoon. I came out earlier this evening, and she was standing in the corner and wouldn't eat. She was coughing and slobbering a bit. I thought she had a touch of pneumonia, so I penned her up, and gave her a shot of Combiotic. She kept getting worse. I got worried and came out to check on her after Jay Leno went off. She was up but wouldn't move, and was really having a hard time catching air. That's when I called you."

Jay Leno of The Tonight Show? I didn't know ranchers stayed up late enough to watch Jay Leno, I thought to myself as I climbed up on the fence again. I looked around the lot. A group of fat Angus cows, their eyes glowing green in the light, lined the pen's gate, watching the goings on inside the lot.

"Any of the other cows sick?" I asked.

"Nope." Mr. Albright informed me that none of the other cows were having any problems at all.

"Do the cows come in here to graze?" was my second question.

Mr. Albright confirmed that they did, as the water trough that stood along one fence was their only source of water while they were grazing the connecting pasture. I noted a thin tree down the fence line.

"What kind of tree is that?" I asked.

Mr. Albright squinted into the dark, following my pointing index finger.

"A pear tree," he answered. "Them small, hard canner pears. My wife likes to cook with them. She makes a mock apple pie with them, and puts some up in jars." He talked fast, nervously. More information than I needed, I thought tiredly.

"I think the cow may be choking on one," I said, nodding toward the distressed cow.

Mr. Albright's jaw fell open.

"Them cows eat the pears all the time!" he told me. "I've never seen one choke on a pear before."

"You're looking at one now," I said. "Let's catch her head so I can take a look."

With some doubt as to my diagnosis, Mr. Albright signaled his grandson to open the head gate while he went beside the cow to coax her forward in the chute. The cow, stressed from lack of oxygen, stepped slowly forward and moved down the chute to the head-gate. She quietly fitted her head through the head catch of the gate, as if pleading for help. I had retrieved a set of nose tongs from my truck, as well as a powerful flashlight. With the tongs applied to the cow's nasal septum, I hoisted her head, using the overhead bar of the chute as a wrapping post for the rope on the tongs. The upward angling of her head caused the cow to gape her mouth wide. She gave a soft strangled bawl, and attempted to cough. I shined the flashlight's beam down her throat.

There, lodged firmly in the pharynx, pressing heavily against the tracheal opening, was a slobber-covered green pear. I asked Mr. Albright to step over and look inside the cow's mouth to see what I could see in her throat. He nodded grimly, a mixed look of disbelief, chagrin, and relief on his face.

"Now, we have to get it out of there," I intoned gravely, hoping my plan to remove the pear was a good one.

From my truck I procured a heavy metal mouth gag called a McPherson's Speculum. Designed to allow a veterinarian to safely open and work inside a horse's mouth while floating its teeth, the gag had special mouth plates that could be substituted for the horse mouth plates, allowing the gag to be used on cattle. Mr. Albright's eyes bugged as I fitted the awkward contraption to the patient. Once the gag was in place, I was able to prop the cow's jaws wide open, allowing me a measure of safety for inserting my arm deep into the cow's mouth in an attempt to retrieve the pear.

This was one of those times having the small arms and hands of a woman was an advantage. With the cow's tongue working feverishly to displace the mouth gag, I slid my left hand between the plates of the gag, over her tongue, passed the huge cheek molar teeth, to the back of her mouth. My arm was up to the elbow in the cow's oral cavity before my index finger touched the firm, pebbly surface of the hard, green piece of fruit. There was just enough give in the pharyngeal wall to ease my finger past the pear. I hooked my finger behind the pear and began easing it out of the cow's pharynx. The pressure that resulted was just enough to completely occlude the tracheal opening. The cow, alarmed at suddenly being unable to breathe at all, struggled and surged forward.

I stayed with her, praying the head-gate and nose tongs would hold her and prevent her from slamming the heavy metal gag into my head. The cow reared up as far as she could, which wasn't far due to the restraints on her, but as she came down and hit the ground on her front feet, she exhaled hard and the pear, loosened by my finger, blew loose from its moorings and landed right in the palm of my hand.

I extracted my arm from the cow, triumphantly displaying the offending fruit to the owner while the cow took in great gulps of air, reveling in unrestricted breathing for the first time in hours. It wasn't long before we were able to release her from the chute. She gave a little hop as she trotted back to her herd-mates, bellowing loudly with full lung capacity.

❋

Mr. Albright was delighted with the outcome of the call, and so was I. With a promise from him that he would come by in the morning to pay his bill, I left the Albright Ranch to head back home to my bed and sleeping husband, leaving my happy client and his grandson picking up pears from the lot by the glaring floodlights and handheld flashlight.

Chapter Thirteen

Mr. Carter's Eyesight

The soul is the same in all living creatures, although the body of each is different. ~Hippocrates (philosopher)

Thankfully, not that many calls came in the dead of the night, waking me from much-needed sleep and leaving me weary the next day. A good portion of the emergency calls came during the week, during regular daytime working hours. I had a set of good working pens at the clinic, and if possible, I had the owner bring the sick animal into town where I could exam her and work on her more easily. If the cow had to stay at the clinic for further treatment in the following days, there were good clean stalls to house her, with a chute to help guide the cow from the stall to the squeeze chute for treatment. Many people liked the idea of leaving the animal with us for treatment to over having to deal with a sick cow on the home ranch. Not really surprising, my older clients were often the most willing to make use of that service.

The Carters were one of my favorite couple-clients. Well into their eighties, they were both robust individuals with few health problems. They had lived their entire 60+ years of married life on one ranch, a ranch that had belonged to Mr. Carter's parents before him.

The couple maintained a half-acre vegetable garden behind their house, planted year-round with whatever the seasonal crops may have been. The Carters were generous in giving away the garden's vegetables to friends and family, and would can or freeze much of the produce for their own use later on. I was the happy recipient of many of a bag of sweet corn, turnip greens, tomatoes, peppers, and other good home-grown vegetables.

They kept a flock of chickens for eggs and meat, a pig to raise for slaughter, and usually a pair of turkeys for the holiday meals. I'm sure eating all that wonderful home-grown produce and livestock, plus the daily work that went into tending it all, helped account for the couple's continuing good health so far into their old age.

Mrs. Carter did suffer from mild heart problems, but even at the age of 85, her hearing was extremely acute and she still could read without glasses. Mr. Carter, at 88, was proud of the fact he used no prescription drugs and could read his Louis L'Amour novels with only a good light source to help him see the print on the pages. However, he did have a hearing problem; he was profoundly deaf, actually. His hearing aids were basically useless, and you had to yell loudly for him to hear you. He could manage to hear Mrs. Carter's voice well enough, it seemed; maybe he could read her lips, or maybe his hearing was attuned to the timbre of her voice. If he came in to the clinic without his wife, we usually had to write notes for him to take back to her, to convey findings of my examination of an animal, for medication directions, or whatever else we had to tell her, such as thank you for the bags of produce she inevitably had her husband deliver to us.

Their one son and one daughter had no interest in ranching; it was a sure thing that when the elderly Carters passed away, their herd of 70 or so cross-bred momma cows and two good Brahma bulls would be sold and the ranch land divided up and sold. There was something sad about that, to me. All those years of work, all that dedication and love for the land and its gifts, at the end it was all reduced to paper work and sold in parcels. In the meantime I could do what I could to help them keep ranching.

This particular visit to my clinic was with a large mottled black cow with a bad udder. She was a relatively old cow; the Carters tended to keep their cows until they died of old age. Mr. Carter would just have soon have sold the non-producers as feed them, but Mrs. Carter firmly believed that a cow that had produced a calf for them year after year until she was too old to raise a calf deserved to live out her life on the home place. I knew they had at least one Jersey, well into her 20s, chewing cud in peace in a pasture behind the house, barren for at least the preceding five years. Bulls came and went, but the cows stayed on.

The cow presented to me this day had to be at least 16 years old. She was fat and shiny and was nursing a rowdy bull calf. Her problem was evident as she walked calmly off the trailer, down the loading ramp, and into the holding pen behind my clinic. She was subdued and panting as if with a fever, and had that faraway, preoccupied look suffering animals tend to get. Both of the rear quarters of her generous-sized udder were swollen, red, and painful to look at, the teats strutted and sticking almost straight out to the sides. Not a pretty picture. The cow, graced with the name of "Bonnie" by her loving lady owner, walked slowly, carefully, to avoid striking the blistered-looking udder with a hind leg. After a cursory exam in the holding pen, we urged the suffering cow down the chute to the head gate.

Once the cow was secured in the iron-pipe squeeze, her head restrained by the head-gate, I was able to get a better look at her condition. She had a fever of 105 degrees, no doubt a result of the infection in the rear quarters of her udder. When she had called to schedule an appointment for me to see the cow, Mrs. Carter had told me that Bonnie hadn't been eating well, and it looked like the calf wasn't getting much to eat. Both of these symptoms were common in lactating cows with fevers.

Though Bonnie was a gentle cow by nature and by upbringing, the tendency to kick due to pain was nonetheless there, so I applied a thick, soft rope to the cow's hind legs as a hobble. This simple device allowed me to exam the udder in relative safety.

While still stooped next to the cow, gently feeling over the udder, I called out to Mr. Carter. "She's got mastitis!"

No response. Mr. Carter just stood there silently, watching me work with the cow. I realized my back was to him, and deduced he couldn't hear me and didn't know I was speaking to him. I stood up and turn to him.

"She's got mastitis!" I repeated to him.

Mr. Carter looked a little bewildered. He cupped his right hand over his ear to make a funnel to help take in sound. "Uh?" he asked.

"Mastitis!" I yelled, having raised my voice an octave while pointing at the cow's angry udder. "Infected!"

Mr. Carter nodded in understanding. He'd had cows in the past with infected mammary glands. He knew what mastitis was.

"I figgered as much!" he replied, nodding. Like a lot of deaf people who could not hear even themselves, he spoke loudly. "Can we save her?"

This particular cow was one of Mrs. Carter's favorites. She had bottle-fed the cow from calfhood, and raised her as a pet. Even if the treatment ended up being involved and expensive, Mrs. Carter would agree to it to save the cow. Mr. Carter, on the other hand, did not like treating sick animals; he'd just as soon dispose of her. I figured he would have to hash that out with his wife.

"I think so," I told him. I pantomimed holding a telephone receiver to my ear. "Let me call Mrs. Carter, talk to her, find out what she wants to do." Mr. Carter understood what I was trying to say, even if he couldn't hear me. He tended to leave the decisions on what to do with the cows up to his wife. We left the cow where she was, and headed into the main clinic to the phone.

I called Mrs. Carter, and told her my findings on the cow. As I had assumed, there was no question about treating the cow. Mrs. Carter didn't feel well herself, though, and wanted to know if I could keep the cow for a day or two, do the treatments at the clinic. At home, she'd be the one to treat the cow as Mr. Carter didn't like that job.

"Of course," I told her. "No problem."

I would send Mr. Carter home without the cow. We'd keep the cow and treat her condition for as long as necessary. I felt certain we would see a big improvement in her udder's health within 24 hours, and we could send her home in two or three days. Mrs. Carter had been agreeable to that.

I told Mr. Carter what I had discussed with his wife as best I could by talking loudly and using pantomime. The message conveyed, the old man climbed into his pickup and left for home, leaving the cow, along with her calf, at the clinic for treatment.

The best way to treat mastitis, besides antibiotics, is to strip all the milk from the affected quarters, if possible. Depending on the severity of the case and the cooperation of the patient, it might be an easy job, or it might not be. Bonnie the cow proved to be very cooperative, and her condition, as bad as it looked, was not terribly severe. I was able to milk her rear quarters dry of several quarts of thick, purulent, blood-tinged milk.

With the removal of the bad milk, the relief to the cow was obvious. Since the two front quarters were not infected, the calf would be able to nurse her from them. Once we got the fever down, the cow would begin to produce enough milk for the calf quickly. After I had removed as much of the infected milk from the cow's rear quarters as I could, I treated both the infected quarters with a medication injected with a soft plastic cannula up the teat canal into the udder. I slathered a lanolin-based udder cream onto the stretched skin of the udder to soothe it and relieve the dry skin. I then used an injectable antibiotic to treat the systemic infection raging in the cow. I felt sure that her fever would be down and that she would be eating and producing milk by morning. We put both the cow and the calf in one of the clinic's livestock stalls for the night, providing them with water and hay.

Sure enough, the next morning Bonnie the Big Black Mottled Cow was bright, alert, eating heartily, and nursing her hungry calf. We walked her down the chute and into the head-gate. This time, no foot hobble was necessary to examine the udder, which was more normal in color and obviously not nearly as painful. Nevertheless, I had to milk the rear quarters dry again. Blood and infection was still present in the milk, so I repeated the antibiotic treatment. We would keep the cow for a full three days, treating the udder twice a day during that time after milking her dry. By the third day, the udder was soft and painless, the milk clean and white and infection free. The calf was obviously getting plenty to drink, as the cow was allowing him to nurse from the rear quarters as well as the healthy forequarters of her udder. I decided the cow would be ready to go home after one more treatment that evening.

I called Mrs. Carter to tell her the good news. She was overjoyed. A gentle, sweet lady, she wept a little with happiness for her cow. She promised Mr. Carter would be by the next morning with the trailer to fetch the cow, and to pay the bill. I thanked her, and hung up the phone.

The first person to appear at the clinic the next morning was Mr. Carter with his livestock trailer. He had carefully and expertly backed it up to the loading chute even before we knew he was there. I met him at the trailer to help him load the cow. Bonnie walked sedately and regally up the ramp into the trailer, her fat and sassy calf bucking and snorting along behind her. We shut the trailer gate and secured the latches.

Mr. Carter pulled a checkbook from his pocket. I pointed toward the main clinic, indicating we should go inside to the front desk where my receptionist had his bill ready. Never saying a word, he nodded in understanding, and strode into the building with me.

Leslie had his bill ready, and, rather than yell at the old man to tell him the total, she pointed to the bill, turning it to face him so he could read the numbers himself. He studied it a moment, nodded, and clicked open his pen, wrote the check, and handed it over the counter to her. She quickly wrote the check number on the receipt, and handed it to him. He studied that a moment before folding it carefully and sliding it into his pocket.

Most of the transaction had been performed

without a word being spoken. Mr. Carter was obviously not quite ready to go, though. He had a question from Mrs. Carter.

"Wilma wants to know when she can bring a cat by to be fixed," he said to me. "She told me to ask you that just before I left the house. She would have called, but she said I could ask you the question when I came for the cow."

"OK," I said. "We can give you a date for the surgery."

"What?" he asked.

I raised my voice, looking directly at him. "We can do it on Thursday!"

He cupped his hand behind his ear. "What?" he asked again.

I didn't want to shout any louder. I didn't figure he would be able to hear me anyway. Instead, I picked up a note pad from the desk, along with a pen, and started to write the surgery date for the cat on the paper. Wouldn't you know, the ink gave out before I'd written two letters of the note. I pitched the empty pen in the trash can, and reached for another one from the pen holder on the desk. For some reason there were no ballpoint pens in the can.

After pawing through the assortment of markers and pencils, I grabbed a Sharpie, a black medium point pen, out of the pile. It was well used and the tip was blunted badly. On the paper, the letters ran into blobs unless I wrote them large and blocky. I sighed in minor frustration, and wrote the note in large and blocky letters; a date, a brief set of instructions on not feeding the cat the night before the surgery and what time to have her at the clinic. I placed the note up on the counter in front of the patiently waiting Mr. Carter.

The old man picked up the note, carefully held it up, and read it top to bottom. I could see his jaw tightening, his face going a little red. What was the problem, I wondered? Was it a bad appointment date?

Suddenly Mr. Carter slammed the piece of paper down onto the counter. I jumped, Leslie jumped. Keeping his hand down hard on the paper, Mr. Carter leaned over the counter, glaring directly at me. I drew back a little. He picked the note up in his fist, and shook it violently at me. I cringed.

"I'M DEAF!" he bellowed at me. "NOT BLIND!"

With that he crumbled up the note, thrust it into his shirt pocket, turned, and stomped out of the clinic.

I looked at Leslie in amazement. Obviously, I had offended the old gent by writing the note in big, bold primary school letters. I surely had not meant to insult him.

The next time I saw the Carters was the following Thursday when they brought their cat by for surgery, and Mr. Carter was just as friendly as he had ever been. Mrs. Carter told me that he had come home with the cow that day very upset over the note for her I had written in the big block letters. While she thought it was funny, he obviously had not agreed. He was very proud of not having to wear glasses to read, she said, and that note just got him angry.

I guarantee to you, I never wrote another block letter note for Mr. Carter. I think I even made a point of using a fine point pen to write any notes to him after that. I also made sure there was always an ample supply of working ballpoint pens at the front desk.

✳

You just never know what might upset an individual, that was for sure.

Chapter Fourteen

The Drummond Calves

Be sure you know the condition of your flocks,
give careful attention to your herds. ~Proverbs 27:23

East Texas' winters tend to be erratic in behavior. Every day is different; you just don't know what you are going to get. Snow is a rarity, but it isn't really missed by the East Texas natives. Besides, if it ever did snow, the snow wouldn't have a chance of staying on the ground long, if at all. The unpredictable flights between cold and warm did not allow for a northern-style winter. In this part of the state, one day might be clear and blue-skied, with low humidity and warm temperatures. The next day might be raining and bone-chilling cold. Often a morning would have dark hovering clouds and dank, cold air, then by mid-afternoon the weather would have summer-like temperatures and humidity so high you feel that swimming through the air would be easier than trying to walk. It is not uncommon for homes and businesses to have both heaters and air conditioners up and running within the same 24-hour period. The old saying is, "If you don't like Texas weather, just wait a minute," and it's true.

On cold, rainy days it should have been allowable to stay at home with a wood fire taking the bone-eating damp out of the air, a cup of coffee steaming on the end table as you nestle on the sofa with the cats and a good book. At least, that's what I believed.

However, for a veterinarian who practiced large animal medicine, that option wasn't part of the deal. When a client called, you bundled up in your insulated overalls and rubber boots, pulled on your wool cap, sucked in your gut, and walked out into the weather to your truck to make the drive to the rancher in need of assistance.

One gloomy, late winter morning it was a call out to the Drummonds' ranch, about 35 miles from town. Maureen and Archie Drummond had a small herd of commercial cattle with a Brahman bull as the herd sire. The calving problems tended to be few and uncomplicated at their place, but this wasn't a calving call. This time it was to examine two suckling calves with profuse diarrhea. According to Archie in his call to my office earlier, one calf appeared to be close to death, the other down and so depressed as to ignore anything done to her. The diarrhea was described to be whitish in color and foul in smell. Both calves were from first-time heifers, meaning they were the first-born calves of those two mother cows.

Calving had apparently been uneventful, and the two-month-old calves had been thriving and doing well until this morning. Archie had found the first one lying on the remnants of one of the round bales of hay that he had fed to his herd the day before. The second calf he had discovered standing humped up and droopy later in the day when he had returned to the field with another round bale to feed the mother cows. He had carried both calves back up to the barn lot before calling me for help. I bundled up in my warm vest and rubber boots and headed out the door.

When I got to the ranch, Maureen was at the gate to open it for me and directed me toward the barn where her husband waited with the calves. I drove across the field toward the barn, the cold misting rain keeping my truck's windshield wipers in business. Archie had both calves outside and away from the barn, on a slight hill, which appeared drier than the rest of the pasture. He had placed a plastic tarp on the ground. On this he had heaped clean, dry hay, laid the calves on the hay, heaped more hay over them in fluffy mounds for insulation, and dropped a canvas tarp over that to protect them from the elements. Three cows stood next to the tarp, bobbing their heads so that it appeared that they were trying to peer under the edge of the tarp, looking for their calves. I drove my truck up next to the tarp, cut the engine, and got out. The chilly rain beat a soft tattoo on the canvas tarp laying over the calves.

"I got them as dry as I could, Doc," Archie said, peeling back one corner of the tarp to show me the patients. He gestured toward the barn, set back a little down a slope. "The barn's flooded from that last big rain; nowhere dry in there. I thought this was better."

"This is fine, Arch," I said, kneeling down in the hay next to the calves. Besides the two he had told me about, I noticed a third calf lying under the tarp. It was larger, older, and in better condition than either of the first two. I looked at Arch questioningly.

"I found that little bull calf right after I called you," he explained. "He's got the scours, too, but he doesn't look too bad. I almost missed seeing him. He was kinda dragging along after his mama, and when she stopped, he went to nurse her. I thought he was OK, but then he shot a stream of diarrhea out behind him six feet, I swear. You can see it all over his butt; looks just like these two. So I brought him up, too."

I nodded in understanding. The sicker of the first two calves was a little heifer, a red baldy that smelled badly of diarrhea and death. She was dehydrated and bony, probably weighing no more than sixty pounds. She was flat on her side, heaving for air, her head thrown back and eyes rolled up so only the whites showed. A check with the digital thermometer revealed a body temperature so low it did not register on the device. I shook my head. Her prognosis was pretty grim. The other calf was also a heifer, but she was positioned on her chest, her head turned into her flank. A little heavier than the first and not quite as dehydrated, she appeared to be asleep, and swung her head around slowly in response to my touch to exam her. Her nose was crusty and red, and the nostrils pinched closed and open again rapidly as she breathed. Her rectal temperature was a screaming 106 degrees Fahrenheit. White diarrhea, dried to a yellow hue, stained her rear and tail, while a steady stream of it leaked from her anus. The smell under the tarp was unpleasant to say the least.

The third calf, a gray bull calf that probably weighed about ninety pounds, was bright-eyed and watchful, though that he was also sick was obvious. He lay on his chest, head up and ears forward. He panted from a fever, and when he grunted in protest to being handled, the effort caused foul diarrhea to pour from him. Outside the tarp, the three mother cows waited anxiously. Only the third calf's mama appeared to have been nursed recently. Her udder had a relaxed, somewhat deflated look, versus the other two cows, whose udders were strutted with milk, the skin shiny and red from the strain. Both of those cows shifted their weight from one rear leg to the other, lowing softly from the discomfort of the udders and the concern for their offspring. I turned back to the calves. I had my work cut out for me.

Maureen Drummond had come up to the barn area from the house, a plastic poncho covering her round figure against the misting rain and chill. She offered me a ceramic cup of hot, steaming coffee, which I accepted readily. It was going to be a while in the damp outdoors, administering treatment to these calves. The hot coffee would help make the experience more bearable.

From the description of the calves Mr. Drummond had given me over the phone, I had figured dehydration to undoubtedly be part of the calves' problems. To remedy that symptom, I had loaded a case of liter bags of intravenous fluids into my truck before starting out for the ranch. Now I got up from the ground where I had knelt to exam the calves. I walked to the pickup to set up an intravenous set for each calf. I rigged three bags with IV tubing, selected an IV catheter for each calf, and got my battery-powered hair clippers out. I returned to the tarp-draped calves, and with the clippers shaved a patch of hair from the neck of each calf, just over the jugular vein. After giving a quick scrub to the shaved area, it was time to set the catheters. The weakest calf was most in need of the life-saving fluids, but her condition was so poor, any attempt to try to save her life was possibly futile. I looked up at Mr. Drummond. He was kneeling down next to the calf with me, waiting to help in any way I asked.

"She's pretty bad, Archie," I began. "This may be just a waste of my time and your money to try to save her." Bad as I knew that sounded, I considered it wrong not warn an owner of the costs about to be incurred in the medical treatment of an animal. As a veterinarian and also as a compassionate human being I hated to see something suffer and die needlessly, but I also understood the economics of cattle raising.

Mr. Drummond pressed his lips tightly in thought. His eyes scanned the ailing calf, taking in her labored breathing and sad condition. He placed a hand on her cold shoulder. "Well," he said carefully. "With treatment she might die anyway. But without treatment she'll die for sure. If she lives, I might be able to make up the cost later. If she dies, it's just a lesson learned." He sat back on his heels. "Go ahead and treat her," he said firmly. "We gotta give her the chance."

I nodded, and carefully set the IV catheter into the jugular vein. Within minutes, the fluids were rushing down the plastic tubing from the bag into the calf's system. I handed the bag to Maureen to hold above the calf while I set catheters in the neck veins of the other two calves with Mr. Drummond's help.

In short order, we had fluids running to each of the three calves. Maureen held up the two bags with the lines leading to the two sicker calves while Mr. Drummond held the third bag aloft with one hand, the other hand putting pressure on the rowdy third calf to prevent it from struggling to escape. I prepared antibiotics for injection into the bags of fluids for each calf. It wasn't long before the first calf's bag was almost empty.

"We'll probably end up giving her three liters," I told the Drummonds, indicating the first calf. I pushed the liquid antibiotic into each of the bags of IV fluids with a hypodermic needle and syringe.

"I think two liters will be good for this calf, and one will be sufficient for Bronco Billy there," I said as I stepped back from the procedure. I noticed Maureen grimace in discomfort from having to hold the two bags of fluids aloft. I took one from her, and she smiled gratefully.

"Sure would be good to have an IV stand," I jokingly said, looking around at the treeless terrain.

A light sparked in Maureen's eyes. "We could use the tractor," she said, pointing toward a large green machine parked across the field. It had a front-end loader, plus a hay spear on the back. "We can hang the bags on the loader. It has hooks on it."

"That's a great idea," Mr. Drummond said, bouncing to his feet and handing his wife the bag he had been holding high over his calf. "I'll go get it."

He trotted across the field toward the tractor and climbed into the cab. In a minute, the tractor roared to life, farting a plume of exhaust into the chilly air. It bucked in place as Mr. Drummond popped it into gear. He angled the machine toward us and the calves, raising the bucket on the front high as he approached us.

The two sicker calves paid no heed to the approaching mechanical monster. The third, livelier calf made a half-hearted attempt to rise up under my steadying hand on his withers before he settled down into the hay again. The great diesel tractor blatted its way over to us, looming huge and smelling of fuel and oil. The bucket dropped slowly until the lip hovered about shoulder height above us and the calves. Two chain hooks were welded to the upper edge of the bucket. Cutting the tractor engine, Mr. Drummond climbed down out of the cab, and came around to scrutinize the placement of the machine, tipping the bucket so it faced downward, leaving space for the IV bags to be hung from the hooks on the upper edge of the bucket. He lowered the bucket down a few inches to allow easy access to the hooks. Satisfied with that arrangement, he took one of the bags of IV fluids, and carefully hooked the handle of it onto one of the hooks that protruded from the front-end loader bucket. As it swayed gently, he took another bag and did the same thing, while I hung the third bag.

Now we had three calves lying side-by-side, plastic tubing stretching from their necks to the IV bags that swung from the bucket of the huge machine as it stood with authority over us. Freed from holding the bags, Maureen rubbed her arms gently to remove the fatigue, then gathered up our coffee mugs. Mr. Drummond settled down next to the strongest calf, and I went to prepare some medication to leave with the Drummonds for treatment of the calves over the next few days.

Maureen said she would be back in a minute with fresh coffee. She took off in a hurried walk for the house. Mr. Drummond assessed the arrangement of tarps, then began to rearrange the top tarp, so that in a few minutes he had suspended the tarp from the tractor's front-end loader. Now, we could sit under the cover, out of the misting rain, while tending the calves.

After replacing the empty bags for new ones, I was adjusting the administration rates of the fluids running into the calves when the first and weakest calf showed her first response to the treatment. As the fluids had coursed into her, rehydrating her body cells, she had taken on a "fuller" look; the desiccated appearance of her body was fading. As we watched, her neck relaxed and her eyes, which had been rolled up under the lids, descended to allow the irises to show. Her gasping breath became less labored. She blinked.

"Doc?" Mr. Drummond asked. "Does that calf look a little better?"

"She looks a lot better," I confirmed. "We might have something to work with yet."

With care, I repositioned the calf's legs, so that they folded under her, and set her up on her chest. Her head, now loosely hung on her neck, swiveled to her flank and nestled there. Her breathing effort lessened, as she appeared to sleep.

The second calf had responded well to the fluid therapy, and sat up with vigor, eyes bright and alert. When the mother cow, seeing her calf move, lowed gently, the calf bleated in return. This triggered an anxious barrage of lows and moos from the cows, answered with surprisingly loud bellows from the two stronger calves. However, neither calf attempted to stand. After a minute or so, the cows quieted and continued their worried vigil in silence.

Mr. Drummond excused himself for a moment, and trotted down the slope toward the house. He passed his wife as she made her return trip with a thermos of hot coffee. They exchanged quiet words before continuing on their paths. Maureen reached the tractor under whose bucket the calves and I waited, and she handed me a clean cup, uncapped the thermos, and filled it with black, aromatic brew. We silently studied the three patients.

"Both those two bigger calves look good," Maureen observed, nodding at the stronger calves. "And I never would have thought that little one would make it."

We watched as the small heifer began to shiver, her body responding to the fluids, beginning to warm up her system. I knelt down and checked her rectal temperature. 97 degrees. It was still well below the normal calf temperature of 102, but definitely on the rise. I smiled up at Maureen.

"She's coming around," I said.

Mr. Drummond returned from the house shortly, toting three folding aluminum camp chairs. We each took one, and settled under the tarp to continue our vigilance of the patients, sipping our coffee, and making small talk about weather, the price of cattle, pasture maintenance, and other ranch topics.

The big gray bull calf's IV had run dry. He was attempting to stand up, having thrust his butt into the air, one front leg thrown forward. In another second he had gained all four feet. He bellowed strongly at his mother, who answered loudly in return. The other two cows began to bawl at their calves, hoping for an answer. The bigger heifer bleated alertly, and also attempted to rise. I hurried to remove the IV catheter from the bull calf. Now sooner did I have it free of his vein when he bucked strongly under our hands, and surged toward his mother. We let him go. He trotted to her and began nursing enthusiastically, his tail swinging rapidly in arcs. The cow ran her long, raspy tongue over his back. He suckled noisily, his tail flapping with more vigor. We grinned.

The IV was removed from the bigger heifer, and Mr. Drummond and I encouraged her to stand. With a heave, she rose to all four feet. She stood shaking a few minutes before calling to her mother. The cow, anxious to be nursed and be relieved of the milk engorging her udder, bellowed happily. The calf staggered out from under the tarp toward her. Like a newborn, she prodded along her mother's side and flank, seeking the udder, which the cow presented impatiently. The cow gasped in alarm when the calf found the sore udder and butted it, but she did not kick at the calf. She allowed the calf to fumble and find the teat. So eager to be nursed was she that great streams of milk began to run from her udder. What a look of relief she assumed as the calf found the teat and began to nurse, first hesitantly, then deeply and eagerly.

We turned our attention to the last calf, still lying in the hay, an IV dripping clear, antibiotic-laden fluid into her veins. The mother cow, hearing the wet suckling of the other two calves, again lowed at her calf, encouraging it to live. I evaluated the cow's condition from my position under the tarp.

"We need to get some of that milk off that cow's udder," I told Mr. Drummond. "You think we can get her in the pen?"

"We can try," he answered, heaving to his feet and heading for the barn. "She'll usually follow a feed bucket."

In a couple of minutes, he returned carrying a galvanized bucket half filled with range cubes, a type of cattle feed. When the cow heard the cubes rattle in the bucket, she immediately turned her attention from her calf to the bucket. All her attention focused on the metal container. She glanced back at her calf, seemed to note that it did not move or appear in any danger, and stretched her head out to the bucket. Mr. Drummond fed her a single cube from his hand. The cow wrapped her tongue around it, took it from him, and chewed it thoughtfully. With a quick flick of her ear toward her calf, she began to walk after Mr. Drummond as he carefully walked backward, luring the cow to the pen next to the barn. As they passed through the gate, I slipped up and closed it behind the cow. She turned and looked back toward her calf and lowed, long and low. When the calf did not answer, she seemed to shrug, and then once again sought out the food-giving bucket.

Mr. Drummond gave her another cube out of his hand, then turned and walked to the end of the pen, the cow following calmly behind him. He started down the long alleyway of the gathering chute. With just a moment's hesitation, the cow started down the chute behind him. This easy penning was certainly an advantage of gentle cattle that had no fear of their human handlers. I placed a bar behind her to keep her from backing out of the chute. In no time, Mr. Drummond had lured her into the squeeze chute. Since the cow was cooperative and not struggling, we elected to forgo catching her head in the head-gate. We would milk her as she stood in the squeeze chute.

Her bag was tight and sore, but except for only one half-hearted kick, the cow did not object to me cleaning her teats, applying a little skin-softening udder balm, and milking about a gallon of milk from her. As I finished up, the cow stood quietly, eyes half closed in a daze at the relief of the painful udder pressure. Mr. Drummond opened the front of the chute to release her from its confines. He poured the rest of the cubes out on the ground for her to eat. I went back to see how the calf was faring.

I was amazed to see the heifer sitting up on her own, her eyes open and liquid again due to the fluid therapy, her ears pitched forward in alertness. She looked like she had gained 20 pounds, all of it plumping her skin and giving her hair a shine. Maureen sat in her chair, coffee cup in one hand, the other resting on the calf's withers.

"She tried to get up," she reported happily. "Only

she was too weak, and I made her stay still. I think she'll make it, don't you?"

I had to agree. What a couple of hours ago had been a dried- up shell of a creature was now vibrating with life. I carefully removed the IV catheter from her jugular vein, the fluid bag having emptied out. As I stepped out from under the tarp, a dazzling ray of sunshine split the cloudy sky and sent bright light spilling across the ground. Everything, that a moment ago had been cloaked in mist and grayness, sparkled in the sunny brightness like watery jewels and color. A large patch of blue sky blossomed; clouds went from monochrome gray tones to brilliant white. Blades of green grass seemed to suddenly spring from the mud, giving a fresh, vibrant color to the ground. Flashes of blue and red appeared along the fence-row as bluebirds, cheered by the appearance of the sun, made their presence known with gleeful chirping. A flock of crows, cawing raucously, rose from the field beyond, their wings flashing purple-black in the new sun. A gentle breeze cruised low over the new grass, bringing the smell of the coming spring. I breathed in deeply. I felt completely satisfied with my life at that moment.

Mr. Drummond returned to the calf, grinning in surprised joy at her obvious return to the living. With a flourish he threw the tarp up and back, so that the warming sunshine could fall on the heifer. Her coat, not so long ago dry and lifeless now glowed, the red of it gleaming in the light. She suddenly bleated, long and loud. The mother cow, still scooping up the range cubes, jerked her head up in surprise at the sound of her calf, cubes raining from her gaping mouth. She bellowed excitedly, and trotted toward us. With great snuffling breaths, she checked her offspring over stem to stern. The heifer, invigorated, struggled to gain her feet. Mr. Drummond and I sprang to her aid, helping her remain up as she tottered toward the anxious cow. Trembling from the effort, the calf, weakened from her ordeal, nuzzled her mother's flank for the udder. The cow stood rock-still, waiting for the calf's tongue to wrap around one of the teats. It was wonderful to hear the wet sound of suckling, at first slow and weak, then stronger and faster. After just a short time, we were able to release our steadying hands from the heifer. She continued to suckle vigorously for several minutes before becoming exhausted from the effort. She panted, her belly filled. After appearing to think about the situation, she slowly turned and staggered back to the hay on the tarp, folded her legs up, and collapsed into the hay. This time when she folded her head around to her flank, it was in deep sleep, not the stupor of on-coming death.

The Drummonds and I grinned at each other at the pleasure of the sight. What started out as a cold, misty day with death in the forecast ended in a sun-filled afternoon with three calves bounding in life, each with a great chance of survival. Even the smell of sickness had dissipated on the slight breeze that fluttered the edge of the tarp and ruffled the shiny red hairs of the calf. I began to pick up the used fluid bags and other equipment. It was time to head back to town.

I dropped the trash into the truck's disposal can, and looked back at the calf. Bright, long, low beams of late afternoon sunlight lit up the area, making the drops of rain and little puddles of water on the ground glitter. The cow stood contently over her calf, chewing the range cubes being fed to her by Maureen, who had fetched the feed off the ground for the cow. Mr. Drummond worked to remove the no longer needed tarp from the front of his tractor. It all together added up to a very good picture.

*

As I stood by my truck in the warming sunshine, watching the revived calf, hearing the twitter of birds out seeking food for their dinner, listening to the grinding of the cow's teeth on her feed, I knew why I did what I did for a living. It was for moments like this. This peaceful, bucolic scene of contented cows and satisfied owners. This picture of life after such a close brush with death. This result of my education and dedication to life. I breathed in deeply of the crisp, cool, late winter air, and sighed with contentment. I was profoundly grateful to the people like the Drummonds, who called upon me and trusted me to help them with their animals. The will to live and remarkable ability to rebound in creatures such as these calves was simply amazing. I was delighted to be a party in it all. I was happy. At that moment, I couldn't think of any better way to earn a living.

Chapter Fifteen

Dr. Russell and the State Trooper

Why should man expect his prayer for mercy to be heard by what is above him when he shows no mercy to what is under him? ~Pierre Troubetzkoy

Not all my Adventures with cows occurred in the years after graduation from veterinary school. Quite a bit of my experience with cattle was gained while working as an assistant and technician for other veterinarians in the years before I went to veterinary college. Some of those times I remember fondly. Others occasionally spring unbidden from my memory storage boxes, and I relive the event in all its color and sound and texture. Sometimes that's good. Sometimes, it's not so good.

Dr. Frank A. Russell was a tall, lean young veterinarian who came to work at the Twin City Animal Hospital in 1974. He had been hired as an associate to the owner-partners, Dr. Francis N. McClellen and Dr. Greg L. Roberts, my bosses. I had been hired there only a few months earlier as a veterinary assistant/technician. My duties included helping with cases, cleaning, taking inventory, and often working the front desk. Most Sundays found me in the kennels, cleaning cages and feeding the animals that were boarding there, or caring for any patients held over the weekend. I loved my job. Veterinary college was still far into my future.

Once Dr. Russell came on board, it took me awhile to adjust to having three people to answer to, to assist, and to clean up after. I did all right. I lived for the days when I was called upon by one of them to jump into a pickup and accompany the veterinarian on a ranch call. I loved being out in the country, working with the horses and cattle on the ranches that used the Twin City veterinarians. I know I learned volumes watching these men work. I couldn't wait to get to work every morning, to see what else might be happening in the intriguing world of veterinary medicine.

Dr. Russell came in one freezing Sunday morning while I was at the hospital cleaning up after the boarding dogs and cats. He had come to stock his truck with necessary supplies before heading out on a calf delivery call. He asked me if I wanted to go along with him. I had not assisted Dr. Russell on a cattle job at that point. I jumped at the chance. We loaded into his little Chevy S-10 and off we went to Thompson, a small community about 15 miles from the hospital.

Our patient turned out to be an undersized heifer trying to deliver an oversized calf. Something Dr. McClellen would call, "a calf trying to have a cow." Mr. Haverty had the cow in a pen that fortunately was under a roof, considering the stiff, cold wind blowing from the north. Nonetheless, due to recent rains, puddles of iced-over water dotted the soggy ground. The cow had lain down before we got there, and was straining half-heartedly, a steaming puddle of amniotic fluid on the ground beneath her tail. Two white hooves peeked from her vagina as she strained, and disappeared again when she relaxed. Mr. Haverty had thoughtfully stockpiled a stack of empty paper feed sacks to place on the ground behind the downed heifer, to give Dr. Russell a somewhat dry area on which to kneel while he worked.

Dr. Russell reluctantly removed his coat while I fetched the gallon jugs of warm water we had brought with us, as well as the OB sleeves and soap. He was already shivering in the cold air as he slid the crackling plastic gloves on one at a time. He soaped up, then rubbed his hands and arms vigorously, working to raise a lather in the cold air.

"I almost can't wait to get to work," he said, jokingly. "At least it'll be warm inside the cow."

That was one of the good things I was to learn about calf deliveries on cold days. Once you went to work inside the huge warm body of the cow, you didn't even realize how cold it might be outside. With the vet straining and sweating from the exertion of the work whilst armpit deep in a cow, observers might be freezing while they watched and waited to help.

Dr. Russell knelt on a clean paper feed sack behind the little heifer. His initial exam was done quickly. He sat back on his heels and looked up at Mr. Haverty, who stood near the fence with his coat collar turned up against the wind, his hat pulled down firmly on his head.

"The calf is dead," Dr. Russell informed him. "The head's turned back. We're going to have to cut the calf up to get it out."

"What's that going to cost me?" asked Mr. Haverty.

It wasn't a rude or uncommon question. The commercial raising of calves for the beef market was not often a high-paying career. The keeping or selling of a breeding cow was a decision made on economics. If her value as a brood animal that could supply calves for sale was higher than the expense of fixing a problem, then a rancher would gamble on a veterinarian's skill to correct the problem. If, however, the veterinary expense outweighed the cow's current or potential monetary value, in many instances the cow's life was terminated or she was sold as quickly as possible. The profit in cattle production can be so marginal many ranchers will sell a problem cow rather than risk her costing him more later on. The sale barns see many cows brought to market with histories of problems such as vaginal or uterine prolapse, a bad udder, dystocia; anything that might compromise her ability to reproduce and/or raise a calf. Even a non-reproductive problem such as lameness can seriously affect a cow's ability to get around and graze, carry a calf to term, or keep up with the herd. A sick or lame cow is a liability, and will be sold quickly to lessen her drag on the finances of the ranch. I've heard many a rancher say it costs as much to feed a good cow as it does to feed a bad cow, so might as well only feed the good ones. In actuality, a bad cow costs more.

So, when Mr. Haverty asked the cost of removing the dead calf from the cow, he had already calculated the cow's worth as she lay on the ground before him, which was nothing, against her potential if the vet was able to save her. He needed to know if any further expenditure would recoup his losses. If the cow could be saved, he could sell her after a couple months to make up the cost of the procedure. If she could not only be saved but also salvaged as a breeding animal, the veterinary costs would be an investment in future profits.

Dr. Russell closed his eyes and mentally added up the cost of the work to be done. He opened them and faced Mr. Haverty.

"I can get the calf out in one of two ways," he said. "We could do a C-section. It would be fast and the cow would probably recover fine from the surgery, but you'd have to sell her. Her chances of having a calf without a problem later might not be good. If I cut the calf up to remove it with what's called a fetotomy, the cow would have a better chance of having calves again." He stopped, waited for Mr. Haverty to think over what he'd just told him. "The C-Section would cost you about $100.00," Dr. Russell told him. "The fetotomy won't be as much, and the risk is less to the cow."

Mr. Haverty rubbed his chin, staring down at his

little cow that grunted as she strained against the twisted calf inside her. When he said nothing, Dr. Russell spoke again.

"This is her first calf," he said. "She's in good shape now, and she's a nice-looking cow with some growing yet to do. I'd bet she'd go on to make you a good cow. But if you want to sell her anyway, if we did a C-section and she went to sale, you'd just get slaughter prices when the buyers saw her incision. If we do the fetotomy, she'd probably bring a better price at the barn."

Mr. Haverty nodded in understanding. "If we don't do anything, she dies," he mused. He made up his mind then. "Do it," he said. "If you can get it out without doing a C-section, do it."

Boy, was I excited. Though a bit disappointed that I would not get to see a C-section on a cow, something I'd never witnessed, I'd never seen a fetotomy done either. I loped alongside Dr. Russell back to the truck to help get the equipment he would need to do the job. Once armed with the instruments needed for the medical procedure we hurried back to help the cow.

The job turned out to be messier than anything I had anticipated. Dr. Russell had already removed his coat and now took off his sweat-shirt. Not only was he warmed from the exertion of the job, but he also didn't want to get his clothes any nastier than necessary. He resumed work with just a T-shirt to cover his torso. Mr. Haverty kept busy, replacing the wet and dirty feed sacks on the ground behind the cow with clean ones as needed.

Though the calf was dead before the procedure

began, it was still fresh and the blood had not yet clotted in its blood vessels. Bright red blood washed over the doctor's arms as he worked. He had to remove the calf's head and neck, severing it from the body with a long, serrated wire run through a metal tube; a fetotome. The metal tube prevented injury to the cow's vaginal walls as the wire, actually a saw, was worked back and forth through the tissue of the dead calf.

Once the head and neck were separated from the calf's body, it was removed from the cow. After that, Dr. Russell was able to deliver the rest of the calf with only moderate effort in the standard manner. Chains were applied to the front limbs. I worked the lever of the calf puller, with Dr. Russell's instructions, to slowly draw the fetus out of the cow.

Once the remains of the calf were delivered, Dr. Russell removed the already loosened afterbirth from the cow. He placed two antiseptic boluses in her uterus to ward off infection. A penicillin injection followed.

While we carried our equipment back to the truck, the cow, as if suddenly aware she was now longer burdened with the dead calf, stood up. Mr. Haverty was very pleased with the results of Dr. Russell's efforts. He quickly wrote a check for the amount Dr. Russell named.

When Dr. Russell turned back to the pickup, shivering in the cold, I held up his coat to him. He started to take it, but then looked down at his T-shirt and arms, now soaked with blood and the birth fluids.

"That's a new coat," he said. "I don't want to get this stuff all over it. I won't put it on. I'll just turn up the heater in the truck and drive back to the clinic as fast as

I can."

I held onto the outerwear. He folded his long legs up to get into the driver's seat. I ran around and jumped into the passenger seat. We waved to Mr. Haverty as he held the gate for our departure. Dr. Russell cranked the heater knob in the truck over to full power. He was shivering violently as the wet clothing he wore started to dry out from the warm heat blowing from the vents. He threw the truck into gear and we bumped down the ranch lane to the highway. Traffic was minimal on this early Sunday morning on the paved road before us. Dr. Russell jammed the accelerator to the floorboard and the little pickup jumped, screaming, into high speed.

I just held on to my seat, clutching the doctor's coat in my lap. The heater was noisily cranking out warm air and Dr. Russell was leaning over the steering wheel, still shivering. Suddenly, he sat up, staring into the rear-view mirror. "Uh oh," he said, taking his foot from the accelerator.

I twisted around and looked out the back window. Roaring up behind our pickup was a state trooper's black and white car, the red and blue lights on the top flashing. The siren was just audible over the noise of our truck's raging engine and heater fan. As the pickup's screaming engine slowed, we could clearly hear the sirens on the law enforcement vehicle whining shrilly. Dr. Russell let the truck slow down and drifted it to the road's shoulder.

"How fast were you going?" I asked, as the truck bumped over the rough gravel surface of the shoulder.

"I don't know. About 80, I guess," he said, watching

via the rear- view mirror as the trooper stopped behind us. The siren's wail wound down, but the red and blue lights continued to flicker, rotating their colors through the rear window of our truck. The speed limit on that stretch of highway was posted at 65 mph. If Dr. Russell had been doing 80 mph, then we had been speeding, and properly caught at it, too.

"Maybe I can explain it to him," Dr. Russell said. He was agitated, nervous. "Maybe if I explain we just finished a calf delivery, and I wanted to get back fast because I was cold." Without giving me a chance to give my opinion, he wrenched the door handle up and pushed open the door.

I glanced back at the DPS officer, who was not looking toward our vehicle. He had gotten out of his car and was now bending back in, apparently to get his ticket book. Dr. Russell had leaped out of the truck and was taking long strides toward the officer.

The officer was just straightening up while placing his Smokey hat on his head when he looked up and saw the rapidly approaching man. He started, his face collapsing with shock and fear. He dropped his ticket book onto the pavement. He stumbled backwards, clawing at his holster with both hands but unable to unbuckle the flap.

I stared, gape-mouthed. I could see what he could see. He could see a tall, t-shirted man covered with blood almost running toward him. Combined with the intense look in his eyes and the determined set of his chin, Dr. Russell must have looked like a mass murderer bent on annihilating the officer also.

My immediate thought was, "Oh my Lord, I'm going

to see a man get shot." I was sure that any second the officer would get his gun free of the holster. I would see him crouch slightly, both hands gripping the gun. I would hear him yell "Halt!" Only Dr. Russell wouldn't understand, and wouldn't halt. After all, he was just a cold, dirty veterinarian trying to get home fast to clean up and get warm. He just wanted to hurry over and explain the situation to the trooper and go home. The officer wouldn't know that. Dr. Russell would keep up his rapid advance toward the officer, unaware of the mortal danger he was in. The officer would yell "Halt!" one more time. Then he would squeeze his eyes down to slits, his mouth closed so tight his lips would be thin, tense lines. Then he would fire his weapon. It would be horrible. Dr. Russell would be thrown backwards, arms up; his blood bright and wet as it gushed and covered the stains of the calf's blood already drying on his T-shirt. I would be screaming by that time, unable to move. Or maybe I would be screaming while tearing off the truck's door to get out and help my fallen boss. Either way, I would be screaming. I was going to have to start screaming for real any second. Oh my God, I was going to see a man, a man I *knew*, get *shot*!

Thank God, the scenario in my head did not play out there on the highway on that cold Sunday morning.

As the obviously frightened officer back-pedaled, fumbling for his weapon, Dr. Russell threw up his hands and started talking. I could barely hear his voice over the rumble of the truck's engine and the loud hum of the heater's fan. I could see the officer, his face blanched white, nodding vigorously, fingers clenching and unclenching over his holster. I could see that he had unsnapped the restraining flap on the holster. I could see the gun was half out of the holster, too. Dr. Russell was talking loudly, flapping his hands as he explained why he was speeding. The officer kept nodding his head rapidly, and waved Dr. Russell away.

As Dr. Russell gave the officer a thumbs-up and turned back to the pickup, I watched as the trooper slumped, knees buckling, against the side of his car. As Dr. Russell hustled back to the pickup, grinning, I saw as the officer, color creeping back into his cheeks, blew out a long breath, white in the cold air, and staggered upright. He pulled his open car door open a little more, looked down briefly, and got into the car. I wondered if he was checking his shorts for wetness. I wondered if he would report the incident back at the station.

Dr. Russell flung his long body into the driver's seat, slammed his door, and threw the gear lever into first. He popped the clutch, sending the little Chevy hopping down the highway.

"He let me go with just a warning," he told me, totally unaware of the dramatic scene I had witnessed, partly real, partly imagined.

"He almost shot you," I gravely informed him. The truck swerved sharply. I looked quickly back toward the trooper. His car had not moved. The lights were still flashing round and round, red-blue-red-blue.

"What?" Dr. Russell squeaked, jerking his head around to stare at me.

"He almost shot you," I repeated. "Lucky for you, he couldn't get his gun out of his holster."

"Why was he going to shoot me?" Dr. Russell's voice

had gone an octave higher than normal, with a little tremor making it almost musical in quality.

"Look at yourself," I told him. "He probably thought you had just murdered a bunch of people, and he was next."

Puzzled, he glanced down at the front of his shirt. His eyes widened and his mouth fell open in an O. The truck swerved a little again. He plucked at his messy shirt with the fingers of his right hand, his left hand clutching the steering wheel, trying to hold the truck in the correct highway lane. I could see the blood draining from his face as he realized what I said was true, leaving his face even whiter in contrast to the bloody T-shirt.

※

Neither one of us said another word on the way to the vet clinic. I don't know if Dr. Russell ever told the other two veterinarians what happened on that drive back from a bloody calf delivery. I never mentioned it to them. I do know that Dr. Russell never left on a call after that without a clean shirt to change into. And I don't believe he ever, ever, in the following years, got a ticket for speeding.

Chapter Sixteen

Mr. Bryan's Ragged Little Heifer

Because the heart beats under a covering of hair, of fur, feathers, or wings, it is, for that reason, to be of no account?
~Jean Paul Richter

Cattle ranching is an economical venture, for the most part. While some folks get a few cows to putter around with and use on their tax forms, raising cattle for sale is time-consuming hard work that often barely breaks even financially at the end of most years. Calves are generally weaned and sold as soon as possible. Good heifers might be kept back from sale to replace cows that have been removed from the herd or to increase the herd size. Aged or otherwise poor producing cows are usually culled from the herd, sold before they become too much of a liability.

Ronald Bryan kept a large herd of Black Angus cows with a Hereford bull. The cross between the two breeds resulted in a commercially popular calf known as a black baldy, an animal with a black body and a white face. The baldy steers and heifers were usually the best sellers to feedlots, and buyers paid good money to load their trucks with the white-faced calves. Mr. Bryan generally sold all the calves produced in his commercial herd, including all the heifers.

Mr. Bryan also kept another herd comprised of registered Black Angus cows and a good Black Angus bull. This herd, smaller than his commercial one, produced the replacement heifers he put into his commercial herd as the cows aged out, lost production, or were otherwise culled.

I received a call one day from Mr. Bryan to come to his ranch to vaccinate his purebred Angus heifers that he had decided to keep as replacements. He said he had about 30 head of the heifers, just five months old. We agreed on the date and time that I would come. He told me which set of pens on his ranch he would be working the heifers from on that day.

The date of the vaccinations was a beautiful fall morning. Leaves had turned from green to golds and reds, yellows and browns. The air was crisp and clean, the sky a uniform brilliant blue. It was a fine day to work cattle.

Mr. Bryan tended to be a calm, easy-going man around his cows, and the peace he radiated as he went about his work was reflected in his cattle's demeanor. Usually when I went to work cows for him, he was the only one there to do the sorting and moving of the cattle. He was so relaxed in his job that the cattle rarely gave him any trouble.

When I arrived at the ranch that particular day, the heifers were standing quietly in the holding pen. I cut the engine of my pickup and climbed out of the cab. Mr. Bryan strode over and we shook hands solemnly. I turned to survey the heifers in the pen.

They were a beautifully uniform group, each calf the same size and shape as the next. They were fat and slick, obviously well fed and tended. They all had glossy black coats and shiny black eyes with which they regarded us casually. They knew something was up and that the something involved them, but they did not appear alarmed about it. They would be a nice, easy group to guide through the chute.

My job this day was to vaccinate them against the bacterial disease that causes Brucellosis, commonly called "Bang's Disease" after its discoverer. A highly contagious bacterium, its worse effect on infected cattle is late-term abortions in susceptible cows. Prevention of the disease involves vaccinating heifer calves against infection when they are between the ages of four and twelve months. A zoonotic disease, Brucella organisms can also infect humans, causing symptoms known as "undulant fever" in the United States and by other names in other countries. Because humans can contract it, it is a reportable disease, meaning cases of it, human or animal, must be reported to the proper government officials. At the time I was practicing cattle medicine, Brucellosis management and control was a federally and a state-regulated operation in Texas. Only a licensed veterinarian could handle the vaccine and vaccinate heifers against the disease. To show they had been vaccinated officially against the disease, a tattoo was applied to the inside of the right ear of each calf. The tattoo indicated the year and the quarter of the year the vaccine was given, as well as having a V-shield emblem in its center. The V-shield meant a licensed veterinarian had administered the vaccine in the proper manner.

Along with the permanent tattoo, an elongated orange metal tag was stapled to the right ear. The orange tag was an individual identification tag for the heifer. The tags were sequentially numbered, one assigned to each calf vaccinated. The numbers were recorded on an official state form, in quadruplicate. One copy was given to the owner, one was stored in the administering veterinarian's files, and two would be sent to the state offices of the Texas Animal Health Commission in Austin, Texas.

As I mixed the vaccine and set out my syringes, needles, tattoo pliers with its ink and the paperwork on a clipboard with a pen to make the necessary notations, I noticed an odd-man out in the group of calves. Cavorting with one of the black calves at the back of the group was a white-faced red calf. She was much smaller than the black heifers, with a long, rough haircoat that stuck out in all directions. Her hipbones thrust out from her skinny body in sharp contrast to the robust builds of the black calves. I might not have noticed her at all, small as she was, except for the fact that she was bouncing around merrily, butting the other heifers with the tiny horn nubs sprouting on her head. I glanced over to Mr. Bryan, intending to ask him about the heifer, but he was occupied setting up the gates of the chute in preparation of starting the heifers down the alleyway. I figured the red heifer was probably just accidentally mixed in with the black calves. She certainly didn't look like any other heifer I had ever seen produced on the Bryan ranch.

The alleyway to the squeeze chute in this particular set of pens was just long enough to accommodate five calves of this size at one time. That worked out fine for me, as the vaccine I used needed to be mixed in lots of five doses each. Therefore, while Mr. Bryan was bringing up each group of calves, I could be mixing the next vial of vaccine. It always proved to be an efficient way for us to work. In a couple of minutes, five of the little heifers started down the chute, one behind the other in an orderly manner. Vaccinating thirty heifers with such good behavior would be a cinch to get done quickly. Mr. Bryan would send a calf into the squeeze chute where I would catch her around the neck in the head-gate. I vaccinated the first five with ease, the tattoos and ear tags given to each with barely a bawl from any of them. After finishing each calf, I would release the hold of the head-gate on the calf and let her go while Mr. Bryan pushed the next calf forward into the chute. The work was going like clockwork.

When we finished with the first five calves, Mr. Bryan walked back to the sorting pen to get another group of five. As I mixed my next vial of vaccine, I noticed the red heifer charging around the pen, kicking up her heels and harassing the black calves. They appeared undisturbed by her bullying, and continued to walk sedately toward the chute and down the alleyway. I figured Mr. Bryan would sort the little renegade out from the group as we worked.

The second group of five heifers were vaccinated and tattooed as easily as the first group. Mr. Bryan went back for the third round of calves while I mixed my vaccine and put a new needle on the syringe. I watched out the corner of my eye as the little red heifer tried her best to disrupt the orderliness of the process, but the black heifers chose to ignore her, instead paying attention to the tall rancher who urged them down the chute.

As the sorting pen emptied out with each group of five black heifers moving down the alleyway, the red heifer became a little wilder, a little more frantic in her bucking and carrying on in the pen. She would bawl and shake her head menacingly at Mr. Bryan as he moved calmly around the pen. Mr. Bryan continued to ignore her. Each time I looked his way, intending to ask about that heifer, the man would quickly look away.

I was beginning to think this little outcast might be an embarrassment to him. Or maybe he was thinking if he ignored her and just got the black ones to move where he wanted them to, the red one would sort herself out from the herd and he could release her to the pasture without worry about losing the others. Or maybe he intended to keep her in the pen so he could turn her over to the rightful owner whenever he found out who that might be. I sure didn't know, and Mr. Bryan wasn't giving me an opportunity to ask what the case might be.

We were down to the last group of heifers, four black ones and the feisty little red one. As Mr. Bryan directed the little group into the alleyway, the red calf crowded into the space with the black ones. She was third in line, locked between two black heifers in front of her, and two behind her. She was pitching a fit over the confinement, bawling and wiggling fiercely, alternating between trying to barge ahead of the calves in front of her and pushing backwards between the two behind her. The black heifers all ignored her, enduring with grace her wild escape attempts. Mr. Bryan ignored her. I couldn't ignore her. This bony, shaggy little heifer was showing the world her spirit. She was something.

I vaccinated the first two heifers without a problem. I waited to see if Mr. Bryan would tell me to leave the head-gate open to allow the red heifer to go out. "Catch her," was all he said when he caught my questioning look. As she surged forward into the squeeze chute, I deftly caught her neck in the head-gate. She was so much smaller than the other calves that she was able to wiggle her body quite freely in the chute. She bawled and fought the restraint.

Once again, I looked for direction from Mr. Bryan. What did he want me to do with this calf? In answer he diverted his eyes toward the last two calves in the alleyway, and said quietly, "Vaccinate her."

I looked down at the angry little cow-to-be. She got still for a moment, reaching out to snuffle my clothing. I leaned over her and gave her the injection in her neck. She sure didn't like that, emitting a squealing bawl in protest. She resented the tattoo application even more, bellowing in indignation as I swiped the ink over the deep imprint left in her ear by the tattoo instrument. After applying the orange ear tag that had caused the heifer to bellow wildly, I glanced up to Mr. Bryan again, to see him wave his hand to indicate I should release the calf. I opened the head-gate, and she bounded out, kicking once in my direction as she bucked her way over to the other heifers milling around the pen before us.

Without looking up toward me, Mr. Bryan urged the next heifer into the squeeze chute. We finished up the job in another few minutes. I was curious about the red heifer, but it was apparent that Mr. Bryan did not want to discuss it. Since it was his business, I let it go.

As I loaded my supplies into my truck and got out the bill box to make out the ticket for the work done, Mr. Bryan tidied up the area around his pens. He then opened a gate at the far end of the pen the heifers occupied, so that they could return to the pasture beyond. The out-of-place red heifer bounced along with the sedate group of black heifers, a flitting, ragged red contrast to the quietly strolling Angus calves.

I stood watching the calves leave, still wondering about that little red heifer, when Mr. Bryan spoke.

"I suppose you're wondering about that red nothin' calf," he said.

I turned toward him. He was standing easily, his face serene, his hands thrust into his hip pockets as he watched the calves spread out into the pasture.

"Actually, I am curious," I admitted. "She sure doesn't fit into that group."

"That heifer," he began, shaking his head as if in wonder while keeping an eye on her retreating tail. "She was born to one of the old commercial cows I keep in the other herd. I don't recall ever getting a red calf out of one of my good black cows before, but here this little scallywag shows up. The cow didn't want it and wouldn't feed it. I couldn't catch a hold of her, and I figured she'd just die in the pasture, the coyotes getting a free meal." He shook his head again, as if in amazement. "That little rascal survived by going cow to cow and stealing milk."

Mr. Bryan stopped talking for a moment, placing the fingertips of his right hand on his chin, his eyes going soft as he kept them on his little herd. He turned and looked me in the eye, perhaps for the first time that day.

"Anything that wants to live that much," he stated emphatically, "I'm going to let it. She's always going to have a place in my herd. And if you think I'm a little crazy because I keep her, well then, that's just your problem, not mine."

I smiled broadly. "No, Mr. Bryan, I don't think you're crazy at all," I told him. "And that's one lucky little heifer out there."

We stood a moment longer, gazing out over the pasture after the calves. Finally, I turned back toward my truck to leave the ranch. Mr. Bryan solemnly saluted in my direction as I pulled out of his gate. I tipped my imaginary hat in his direction in return, and continued on my way.

✳

I've thought about Mr. Bryan and his little red calf often over the years. I loved the case, loved that the heifer grew up and eventually calmed down, joining his commercial herd and raising her own little feisty red calves in the years that followed. I loved the proof that there are good men out there who don't look at their cattle merely as a means to make a living, but who regard their charges as sentient creatures with their own minds and hearts. Men like Mr. Bryan who were not afraid to honor the animal for what she is, an individual with a will to keep on going in spite of everything against her. This little heifer survived because of her spirit and determination. In her favor, definitely, was her owner, a man who gave her the chance to live and didn't hold her feistiness against her, but rather saw it as an asset to her. In return, the heifer matured, gentled down, and became a contributing member of the herd. I couldn't have come up with a better ending to a story if I had tried.

CHAPTER SEVENTEEN

LITTLE HENRY'S BLOATED COW

*Until he extends the circle of compassion to all living things,
man will not himself find peace.* ~Albert Schweitzer

Convincing some of the older ranchers that I was
capable of doing what was traditionally considered a
"man's job" wasn't always easy. Many a time I ended
up as the veterinarian out on a ranch doing cow work
simply because the cowman was desperate for help
and I was the only veterinarian who answered the call;
the owner's last-ditch effort to save a sick animal. It
certainly wasn't a very satisfying reason to be chosen
to administer medical aid to a cow. However, often
after a successful calf delivery or miraculous "cure"

of a downer cow, I would become the veterinarian of choice the next time the rancher found himself with a situation he couldn't handle without qualified medical help.

It was humorous though somewhat irritating to have some old rancher assume I couldn't do a job because he might think that as a woman I was physically too weak for the work. This, often coming from a man whose body was so bent and broken with age, he could barely shuffle over to the pen to watch the work being done. The work was hard, no doubt about it, but when you get right to the gist of the matter, if a cow doesn't want a man to handle her, regardless of his size and strength, it wasn't going to happen without a fight. One hundred and fifty pounds of human against a thousand pounds of upset bovine is no contest. That's why cattle chutes and head gates, stout ropes, and horses have a place in cattle ranching, and always will. They are used to keep cattlemen safe and to give them the leverage they need to handle the cattle. These things work just as well for a woman as they do for a man, so I unhesitatingly used their available power to aid me in my work.

In a field situation, with no chutes and head-gates available, there is often no way to restrain a cow with anything other than a lariat rope. Knowing when and how to apply leverage comes in handy in such situations.

I got a call one early morning from a rancher with the name of Little Henry Knight. He had gone to his pasture to feed his cattle and had found one cow lying prone, unable to rise. Henry and his two brothers had not been able to get the cow into a sternal (chest) position. At one earlier time, this rancher had had a cow go down and soon thereafter die from bloat. He was in a panic that this cow might soon bloat and die too, and wanted me out there as soon as possible.

Due to a cow's digestive system setup, belching is a highly desirable and necessary result of her somewhat complex digestive process. The rumen, the second of a cow's four "stomachs," is more like a huge fermentation vat than a stomach. If a cow can't belch the gases produced during the fermentation of grass and feed in her rumen, the gases accumulate and cause the rumen to balloon to enormous proportions. The bloated rumen then puts pressure on other internal organs, including the heart, lungs and blood vessels. This pressure will result in the death of the cow if not corrected rapidly.

Any cow can bloat, but a cow lying flat on her side can be in grave danger of bloating. When a cow lies flat on her side, the ingesta in her rumen will move forward and cover the esophageal opening. The fermentation gases produced in the rumen cannot escape up the esophagus and out the mouth as a belch. The down cow will continue to bloat because she cannot belch.

The panic in Little Henry's voice as he reported this emergency with his prone cow indicated he was well aware of the consequences if his down and bloated cow wasn't tended to as soon as possible. I hopped in my truck and drove like a fury to the ranch. A young boy was at the gate holding it open for me so I could drive into the pasture without stopping. The boy pointed into the distance, and far out in the pasture, on a little knoll, was a hay ring, a tractor, and three large men. I drove over the bumpy ground to the group.

As I approached, I could see a hugely bloated black cow laying on her left side, head thrown back and tongue out as she gaped for air. Her eyes bugged from their sockets with the effort of her breathing. Her upper legs were stiff and elevated from the ground and slightly spread from the effects of the distention of her abdomen. The skin of her belly was stretched taut and hard. The three men stood in a circle around her, regarding her with a mixture of pity and frustration. I turned off the truck's motor and got out.

Little Henry stepped forward. He was enormous. He was built like a young bull, and sober in expression. He looked powerful enough to pick the cow up unassisted and set her on her feet. I felt small and puny next to his bulk. His forearms looked bigger around than my thigh, and at 140 pounds, I wasn't a skinny gal.

We shook hands. My hand completely disappeared inside his clasp, and I felt a momentary spiraling of fear, wondering if he would accidentally crush my hand in his. However, his handshake, though obviously capable of fulfilling my perception, was firm yet gentle.

"I hope you can help us," Little Henry intoned in a soft voice that belied the power evident in his body. "My brothers and I couldn't get the cow up. She's too sick to stand."

I turned my focus to the cow. Her neck was arched back and her breathing was ragged. She appeared to beseech the humans who surrounded her to either help her or finish her off. She knew she was dying.

I surveyed the situation. The cow, while bloated

monstrously big, was not herself a large cow, but rather a smallish Angus cross. She was lying close up beside the hay ring, a round, metal pipe contraption about eight feet in diameter built to surround a half-ton round bale of hay and protect it from being trampled by the cattle it was meant to feed. The cow was so positioned that her feet were slightly uphill. Her two ground-side legs appeared to be wedged under the hay ring. From the signs on the ground, the cow had struggled for a while before the bloat caused her to concentrate her efforts solely on breathing. Without assistance, this cow was doomed.

I instructed the men to move the hay ring if they could. Together, Little Henry and his two equally well-built brothers lifted the metal hay ring off the round bale and set it down out of the way. With her feet freed, the cow was still unable to move. She offered no attempt to right herself.

"We need to flip her over," I said. "Her feet are uphill; we need to get her so they are downhill, give her a better chance of being able to get up."

Little Henry, hands on hips, gave me a slightly condescending look. "We already tried that," he said. "Ain't no way we can move her. We were just fixin' to put a chain on her and drag her out with the tractor."

"There's no need for that," I assured him. "We can flip her without it. Easier on the cow, too."

"How?" Little Henry asked, crossing his massive arms over his chest and shaking his head sadly at my ignorance.

"Like this," I said, and stepped toward to the cow. I reached down and grabbed the fetlock of the uppermost front leg. I pulled up on the leg, so that it was sticking straight up in the air. I continued to bring the leg over. The leverage action gently rotated the cow up onto her back and with a little extra effort on my part, the cow continued to roll until she flopped down on her other side. Her feet were now downhill, away from where the hay ring had been.

There's a funny thing that often happens with cows when they are turned over. It's like their entire world changes, shifts focus. That's what happened with Little Henry's cow. Suddenly, her outlook on life rearranged itself, and she decided maybe she wasn't dying after all. With her feet now pointed downhill, rolling up into a sternal position was easy for her. She popped up onto her chest, rested a moment, then extended her neck and belched mightily, the gas trapped in her rumen having found escape up the now unobstructed esophagus. She took a deep, cleansing breath, and belched again.

I glanced up at Little Henry. He and his two brothers were staring, slack-jawed, at the cow. The cow belched again, a long and rumbling belch smelling of wet hay. Her rotund belly deflated remarkably as we watched. This was one cow I would not have to deflate with a stomach tube or trocar. It looked like she was getting the job done herself.

All three of the men moved their dumbfounded gaze from the deflating cow and over to me. As one, and with what appeared to be a great deal of respect, all three of them took a giant step backward away from me.

For a moment I was puzzled by their change

in behavior before I realized what I had just done. Together, these three, burly men had been unable to move the cow an inch. Here I come, a 30-something year old woman, not a body builder by any stretch of the imagination. All I did was reach down, grab a foot, and flip the cow like she was made of paper mache. Leverage is cool.

I let the reaction from the surprised men hover over me for a minute or two longer. Satisfied that my Wonder Woman image was firmly implanted in these men's minds, I explained to Little Henry that this cow had apparently lain down next to the hay ring and got her legs stuck under it. Combining that with the slight uphill incline of the ground, she was unable to right herself again and had bloated. I felt sure the cow would recover now that she was upright. And sure enough, while we stood there assessing each other, the cow gave a mighty heave and rose shakily to her rear legs. After a moment, she put out first one front foot and then the other, and stood up. She stood quietly for a minute, then belched again.

I told Little Henry that if he found another cow down and in distress, he should do whatever was necessary to get her on her feet or in a chest-sitting position. Either position would delay bloating and allow a veterinarian time to arrive and give the cow whatever treatment might be needed.

✳

It was a satisfying trip. I had not explained to those nice young men how I had been able to turn the cow over with minimal strength. I wanted that Wonder Woman mystique to linger a little longer. It just goes to show, though, that a person doesn't have to be built like a brick house in order to do a job. And it certainly helps if you know what you are doing. Not to mention that leverage is always at your service.

Chapter Eighteen

The Binghams
(Country Folk)

If a man aspires towards a righteous life, his first act of abstinence is from injury to animals. ~Albert Einstein

Veterinary medicine is still considered, in some circles, to be a man's profession. My veterinary class was one of the first to have more women than men in it, but the ratio of women to men in all the veterinary schools since then has tipped dramatically in favor of women. That doesn't mean women no longer have to "prove" themselves when dealing with the real world, especially in large animal medicine.

Once graduated from vet school, I bought my own practice. After a couple of years of solo practice, I had developed a reputation as a veterinarian who would see any animal, a pet, or a farm animal, when no other vet was available. I answered calls day and night. Sometimes the weather wasn't agreeable. Sometimes the work wasn't. Sometimes the client was nobody's favorite. And sometimes I was actually the only qualified person in town that particular day when the cow went into labor and couldn't deliver.

That's the way it was one weekend morning when a call came from what sounded like an elderly man. They had a cow down and he, his son, and the helpful neighbor from down the road had been unable to deliver the calf. Their regular vet was unavailable for the weekend. Could I come out and help their cow?

Always willing to help an animal in a crisis, I agreed to drive out to the ranch. I got the directions, changed into my summer cow working clothes; a lightweight pair of coveralls. It was fall but in our area of the country I did not often need to dress in heavier clothing in the autumn months. I headed out the door.

It was a long drive out to the ranch, down at least five miles of washed out sandy road. I crawled along at the maximum speed of a snail. I found the place easily enough and drove up to the house. The cow pens were close by. In one pen lay a cream-colored heifer flat on her left side, her belly stretched tight with calf. Surrounding her stood three men appearing to contemplate the heifer's predicament. One was a wizened little old man with a burning cigarette pinched between two fingers of one hand. Another was a brawny young man who must have been the son. The third was an older gentleman who radiated the aura of a retired white-collar worker. As I stepped out of the truck, I saw the three men exchange grim looks. By this time in my career, I'd seen that look a thousand times. It said, "Oh great. A woman. Just when we need a man for the job." I didn't like it, but I was used to getting the look and chose, as usual, to ignore it. The young man approached me first. After exchanging introductions he cocked his head toward the down cow.

"She's been in labor a long time," he said. "We think the calf's still alive. We tried, but we couldn't move it."

"Let me have a look at her," I said. "Then we'll decide what we'll have to do."

I got my soap, water, gloves, and OB lube, and walked over to the prone cow. She was small, maybe 450 lbs and worn out from her exertions. She had a rope wrapped around her horns with the other end tied off to a stout fence post, presumably to detain her if she chose to jump up and run away. But the most she did was roll her large brown eyes at me and stay where she was.

I knelt behind her, pulled on my long plastic gloves, and did a quick clean-up of her rear. A careful but quick examination of her pelvic canal revealed a live calf, its head and feet both presented to the opening, but wedged tight. I decided I could get the calf out without too much trouble by repositioning its head back a little to allow the two forelegs to come out first, with the head to follow behind the knees. A quick glance toward the men revealed sadly wagging heads and grim faces. They apparently were convinced I was useless for this job, since they, three men, had not accomplished anything with their own efforts at delivering the calf. Ah, well.

I returned to my truck for my obstetrical chains and handles, as well as the apparatus commonly called a calf puller. It is a device developed to strike awe in the uninformed and assist in the delivering of calves. When the gentlemen saw the calf puller, they perked up. The calf puller was a gadget and a big one. Men love gadgets and like to think they understand them. Even if they don't understand them, they are nonetheless interested in them. At least for now I had their attention.

"That machine gonna pull that calf for ye?" asked the elder Mr. Bingham, taking a long drag of his cigarette. His fingers were yellow from nicotine. He'd been smoking a long, long time.

"I'll use it if I need it," I answered. "First I have to see if I can reposition the calf, get it in place so it can come out."

"You ain't gonna get it done," the old man snorted. "My boy Bobby and me been tryin' a long time. He's three times 'big as you. It ain't coming out, lessen you cut it out."

He dropped the nub of cigarette into the manure of the pen, and ground it out with his toe. Bobby, standing next to the cow's head, shrugged in embarrassment. He was a beefy fellow, and I felt for this little cow who had endured his attempts to help her.

"We'll see," I answered.

"I've never seen a woman vet before," chimed in Mr. Garrett conversationally, leaning on the fence near Mr. Bingham. "You been doing this long?"

"Long enough," I replied, and added a little more lube to my gloves.

Once back on my knees behind the cow, I inserted one arm, and pushed the calf's head back a little, to allow room for the legs to come out first. Maneuvering a calf in very tight quarters without harming it or the cow can be quite a challenge.

This poor cow had had three men trying to extract her calf by brute force. She was tired, her vaginal canal tissue swollen, and the calf large. It was a miracle to me that the calf was still alive, but he was. When I put my finger in his mouth to test for reflexes, he grabbed on and sucked hard. That made the job a little trickier, a little more daunting. With an already dead calf, you don't have to worry about hurting it. You just have to get the calf out without harming the cow any more than necessary. With a live calf, you had to protect both the cow and the calf from the damage that might occur. I knew I could get the calf delivered in spite of the aura of palpable skepticism coming from the watching men.

In short order, I had one leg chained. I handed the end of the chain with a handle attached over to the young man, Bobby.

"Pull slow and steady," I instructed him. "Stop pulling when I say stop, and hold the pressure unless I say different."

Bobby was a study of concern and concentration. He easily weighed 250 pounds, all of it hard country boy muscle. I hoped he wouldn't pull so hard as to harm the calf.

I need not have worried. Bobby knew his strength and was so concerned about pulling too much I had to ask for a little extra from him. The first leg of the calf eased forward out of the vagina. I looped a chain on the second leg, added some more lube, and eased the second leg out. The calf's head was half out, laying just behind its knees, right where it needed to be. I slicked up my hands with the OB lube, and slid them into the cow. I positioned my fingers behind the calf's ears, and leaned back, pulling gently. With no more than that, I was able to usher the calf's entire head into the sunlight. We both rested, the calf and I, before completing the delivery. Bobby looked on, his face a study of determination. I signaled him to begin a steady, downward pull on the calf's legs. He complied perfectly.

The shoulders of the calf appeared next. The hips were tight in the pelvis, and I called a break in the extraction process. Sometimes with large calves that need assistance in the birth process, the shoulders will deliver, but the hips might be a little wider, causing them to wedge in the cow's pelvis. It was always a worry for me. However, this little calf was ready to get out into the world. With a little twist to position his pelvis just right, he came clear of his momma's body.

"Well, I'll be danged!" exclaimed Mr. Garrett, slapping his thigh. "She did it!"

Mr. Bingham simply sucked on a newly lit cigarette while watching silently. If he was impressed or otherwise surprised at the successful delivery, he said nothing. The calf was alive and already struggling to breathe and move, shaking his head and flopping his long ears. Bobby was grinning ear to ear, delighted to see the wiggling calf, the result of his assisting the birth. He took a rag from his hip pocket and began to wipe the birthing fluids and blood from the calf.

The cow was the concern now, as she was utterly exhausted and still on her side on the ground. I checked her pelvic canal for tears and possible prolapsing tissue. I found no bad damage. Next I gave her some medication to assist in the passing of the afterbirth, and a dose of medicine to help reduce the swelling in the pelvic canal tissue. Sometimes after a difficult birth, the trauma to the cow will result in her becoming paralyzed in her rear legs. The paralysis might last for a day or two. Sadly, occasionally it will be permanent. I moved to the cow's head and took the rope that was attached to her horns and pulled her into the sitting position.

At first, she gave no indication she cared what happened to her, gave no effort to stay sitting up. Bobby picked up the calf and carried it around the cow to lay it near her head. When the little cow saw and smelled her newborn calf, she became very animated. She began to struggle to stay sitting up on her own. She snuffled the calf, reaching toward it with her long tongue. After a couple tries, she was able to raise herself up on shaky legs to tend to her baby. It was a very satisfying feeling, seeing that happen.

Mr. Garrett, the neighbor, seemed to be the most surprised and happy at the results of my work.

"We messed with that cow for over two hours," he

said. "I figured we were going to have to shoot her." I, for one, was glad they did not.

"Well, come on up to the house," the dour Mr. Bingham said gruffly, snuffing out still another cigarette. "The Missus will write you a check."

I carried my equipment to my pickup and cleaned it up. While I did that, Bobby and Mr. Garrett tended to the cow and calf. They got the cow some water and feed and put down some bedding on the wet ground for the calf. It's a pretty sight, a cow humming quietly while licking on her wobbly new calf.

Mr. Bingham waited silently for me to finish putting my equipment away, occasionally sucking on an ever-present cigarette. When I indicated I was done, he turned and led the way to the house. Silently, he held the door open for me. I walked past him into the kitchen, which was warm and smelling of fresh coffee and bread. Mrs. Bingham was standing at the stove as we went into the tidy kitchen, and she turned to greet me with a smile. She was every bit as big and meaty as her husband was small and wizened. Jack Sprat and his wife came to mind immediately when I saw her. Mr. Bingham, another cigarette already burned down to the filter, shuffled into the kitchen. He pulled a cup out of the cabinet and poured himself some coffee while informing his wife, in an almost bored monotone, that I was able to deliver a live bull calf to the heifer, and both cow and calf were doing well.

Mrs. Bingham was pleased with the news. She beamed a smile at me, and asked me to have a seat at the kitchen table. She had a wonderful, kind face, though she obviously had some health problems that kept her in the house and moving slowly about her work. She graciously offered me a cup of coffee, which I accepted. She produced a checkbook, shuffled over to the table, and took a chair across from me. I gave her the sales ticket with the total on it. She studied the ticket solemnly then carefully filled out the check.

As she handed me the check, she looked across the table at me and said, ever so quietly, "After Mr. Bingham called you and asked you to come help with the cow, he hung up the phone and said to me, 'It's a woman vet that's coming out to help us. Reckon she'll be able to do the job?'" Mrs. Bingham leaned over the table toward me. Her eyes had gone hard, small, and mean. Lips that had smiled softly at me a few minutes earlier were now thin and tight. I edged back from her in my chair, a little frightened. Staring me in the eyes intently, she intoned in a dead serious voice, "I never wanted to hit a man so much in my life."

I couldn't help it; I burst out laughing. Mrs. Bingham reared back in her chair from surprise at my response. Little Mr. Bingham, who had ducked behind his wife as she told me what he had said, peeked at me from around her bulk, blushed and gave a tiny smile. At first confused at my laugh, Mrs. Bingham began a slow smile that finally lit up her face, softening her features once again.

"I guess lots of people think you can't do this work, because you're a woman," she said. "But who could help with birthin's better than a woman?"

I smiled back at her, brimming with agreement with her.

✳

I remained friends with the Binghams and was their veterinarian for many years, until both of them eventually passed away from advanced age and poor health. I'll never forget that couple, their son, or the cows that I tended over the years out at the end of that long, sandy road.

CHAPTER NINETEEN

MEN, WOMEN, AND COWS

Animals are such agreeable friends—they ask no questions, they pass no criticisms. ~George Eliot

I had many ranchers amongst my large animal clientele. It pretty much goes without saying that most of them were men. Many of the men had been ranchers for decades, and were up in age at the time I worked for them. There were also a fair number of women in Houston County who owned cattle and ran their ranches on their own. They were single women and they were also wives of ranchers. There were married ladies who co-owned their ranch with their husbands, and often participated fully in the workings of the ranch.

For an example, Mrs. Schmidt was at the pens anytime I was there, taking meticulous notes on the condition and health of each animal. Mr. Schmidt never made a single decision regarding an animal without first consulting his wife. They seemed to enjoy each other's company and worked well together, dedicated to caring for their cattle.

One of my most loyal and favorite women ranchers was an older woman named Pat Carroll. Pat ran a herd of good Braford cattle outside the little community of Kennard. She also produced and baled her own grass hay. She bought alfalfa hay from New Mexico to supplement the winter feed for her cows. Everyone one of her 125 cows had a name that described some aspect of the cow.

Pat's cows were fat, healthy, and easy to work with, reflecting the temperament of their owner. Until a heart condition forced Pat to sell her cows and retire from ranching, the Serenity Ranch was one of my favorite places to go.

Although the sex of a cow's owner never mattered to me, the sex of the veterinarian occasionally did matter to a ranch owner. Oddly enough, it was the women who sometimes didn't like a female veterinarian showing up to work on their cows.

Mr. and Mrs. Conrad Helms ran a registered herd of red Brangus on the far northern edge of the county. The few times I did go there was because no other veterinarian was available for that emergency. Mrs. Helms, who always referred to herself as "Mrs. Conrad Helms," never by her own given name, disapproved of women as veterinarians, or in any traditionally male job. She told me so each and every time I ended up attending a cow for them. She thought women had no business working on "a cow's private parts" in front of men, was what she told me. It was okay with her if I tube-wormed the horses or sewed up an injured dog. Any time I stepped behind a cow, however, she would tut-tut in disgust that I should be so brazen as to put my hands on the reproductive organs of a bovine. However, I couldn't figure out any other way to deliver a calf or fix a prolapse without touching the cow's vagina.

Finally, after one difficult prolapse repair for which there were several male observers, Mrs. Helms had had enough of my blatant disregard for basic decency. As she gave me the check for the work I had done, she told me in no uncertain terms it was to be the last time I was to set foot on that ranch. Her husband could only shrug his shoulders in helpless agreement with her. I never did go out to that ranch again, and to make the break final, Mrs. Helms had all her cats' and dogs' medical records sent to another veterinary office. An office in which men only worked as the doctors was more suitable for her.

The Langleys were the other extreme from the Helms. Mr. Langley could not be bothered with the cattle. Mrs. Langley, who insisted I called her by her baptized name of Doris, did all the cattle work, while Mr. Langley stayed away from the pens, preferring to tinker in his machine shop. Doris preferred my coming out to her ranch over any male veterinarian. She said I had more compassion and cared more the animals than did my male counterparts. We rarely had any problem handling her cattle.

I'll not soon forget Joe and Fanny Peters. Joe was the cattle owner in that pair. I was called out one day to deliver a calf. Joe said the calf's head was out, but that was all. "It looked dead, too," he said. "If you could come as soon as possible, I'd appreciate it. I don't want the cow to die."

I assured him I'd be there as soon as I could.

When I arrived at their little ranch, Joe had the cow in his good pipe corral. There certainly was a problem, as the bloated head of an obviously deceased calf showed from the cow's vagina.

We sent the cow down the chute, and barred her up behind her rear legs, to prevent her from backing out. With soap and gloves, I examined the cow, trying to determine where the feet of the calf were.
Due to the grossly swollen head of the calf, it was difficult to find the calf's feet. Even if I had been able to locate them, it was apparent that the head of the calf would have to be removed first.

"I'll have to cut the head off the calf first, Mr. Peters," I said. "Then I'll be able to straighten the legs, and pull the rest of it out."

"Do what you gotta do," Joe replied, shaking his head at the sordid idea of it.

About that time Fanny Peters appeared from the direction of the house. "Is she going to be all right?" she asked, standing next to me wringing her hands. I reached into the equipment box of my truck to retrieve the sharp dissecting knife with which I would remove the calf's head.

"I'm sure she will be fine, as soon as I get this calf out of her," I replied, testing the blade of the knife for sharpness.

Fanny was a very sweet woman. She had a cat named Penny, a patient of mine I saw regularly at my clinic. While Joe considered cats to be parasites on the human species, Fanny adored her orange and white cat with a passion. Any little thing that looked out of place in the cat's health had Fanny banging at the clinic door, frantic for help. Often her cause of alarm was nothing serious; a hairball, a case of ear mites picked up from the barn cats that ran wild at their ranch, maybe fleas. I enjoyed her as a client, as her concern over the cat's well-being was based on her true affection for her cat. I walked back to the cow with my knife in hand. Joe was at the chute, and he stood to one side, holding the cow's tail out of my way. Fanny timidly moved around to get a view of what I was about to do to the calf.

"Fanny! Get back!" Joe ordered in a gruff voice. Fanny, startled, jumped a little, and immediately backed up a few steps.

"Go on up to the house!" Joe snapped, trying to hold onto the cow's tail while attempting to block his wife's view of the cow's nether end. "This isn't anything a lady needs to see!"

I paused, knife raised, and looked at Joe in surprise. He turned back to me, having sent his wife scurrying back around the barn toward the house, and saw my expression.

"Oh, Doc!" he said. "I didn't mean you weren't a lady!" He turned to see his wife disappear from view. "I just meant someone like Fanny doesn't need to see

something like this!" He was blushing furiously.
I positioned the knife for my first cut behind the dead calf's head, and said nothing.

"You know what I mean, don't you?" Joe continued, trying hard to explain himself, trying hard to pull that foot out of his mouth, trying hard to apologize for his belief in there being a difference between his wife's status as a lady, and my status as a lady veterinarian.

"Mr. Peters," I replied, deftly removing the calf's head at the first neck joint. "Don't worry about it. But maybe you ought to let Fanny see one or two things like this. Then she'll be more capable in helping you out in such cases."

"Well, as long as I can find a man to help me, she doesn't need to be involved in these things," he responded, obviously without thinking. When it did occur to him what he had said, he blushed again. "I don't mean to say you're a man," he stammered. "It's just that you're a professional. It's okay for you to see these things."

"Good thing, too," I replied. "It's hard to do this with your eyes closed."

The Peters remained loyal clients of mine for the years that followed. When Joe Peters became ill and was unable to tend the cows he loved, Fanny took over the chore and learned to love the cows and the work involved. Then her husband unexpectedly passed away one night, leaving the small ranch in Fanny's care. She continued to live at the small ranch until she remarried a man who shared her love of the land and the cattle.

Her new husband enjoyed the company of her cat, which motivated Fanny to adopt any cat or kitten needing a home, food, and love. To witness her confidence and enjoyment of her life as a ranch owner always caused me great joy when I visited that small ranch to render veterinary care whenever Fanny called for help. It was a good ranch to have to visit and work for.

✳

Over the years, respect for women in traditionally male roles such as ranchers, farmers, horse trainers, and veterinarians, to name a few, has increased significantly. Men in those jobs appear to have come to regard women as equals, as they should. It makes going out to do the work on a ranch, farm or stable much easier, not only for the professional called upon, but also for the animals that require the attention. That is a the overall good result of the persistence of women in doing the jobs they love.

CHAPTER TWENTY

NEITHER RAIN NOR HAIL

Cows are amongst the gentlest of breathing creatures; none show more passionate tenderness to their young when deprived of them; and, in short, I am not ashamed to profess a deep love for these quiet creatures. ~Thomas De Quincey

The longer I worked in Houston County as a large-animal veterinarian, the more I came to realize how many women there were in the ranching business.

These women were not sunburned, tobacco-chewing, hard-ass ladies with a vendetta against men as often seen in old western movies. No; they were, for the most part, kind, considerate, and hard-working individuals. They were black and they were white; they were wives and mothers and often grandmothers; they were young and they were elderly, as well as all ages in between. They were country women who had lived on their ranches all their born days, and they were women who moved to the country to fulfill a dream of owning a ranch of their own. They were educated, intelligent people who happened to be women who happened to like cattle.

I tended many cattle belonging to these women, called upon because I was not only willing to do the job, but because I understood the women's desire to be involved in such a hard job as ranching. I had empathy for the cattle, which the women appreciated, and I had empathy for the women, who were often underestimated for their ability to do their jobs as ranchers in a male-dominated profession.

On one early spring day, I was called out by one of these women ranchers to help with an emergency calf delivery. A lot of my work with cattle was emergencies, and a lot of the emergencies were calf deliveries. Calf deliveries can be quite an adrenaline rush, sometimes long before you get out to the ranch were the cow is. Add some interesting weather, and the day can get very, very intense.

We were expecting a bout of heavy rains this early spring morning. It was still cold enough to require heavy coats. There were occasional torrential rains, which were sometimes preceded by hail, sometimes followed by flooding. An office job, under a good roof with a cup of good, hot coffee on a coaster near your elbow, you sitting in a comfy chair in a climate controlled environment, sure did seem like a better deal on such days. While I had an office, with a coaster on my desk for my drink cups, and even an armed chair to sit in, during calving season that chair in that room didn't see me too often.

On this particular day the weather was not particularly warm, with heavy clouds to the north. Away in the distance, somewhere under the clouds, came a damp muttering of thunder. I stood at the office window, a coffee cup in my hand, hoping the cows of the county could control their labor urges until the storm could pass by. So far, we'd had a quiet morning, cow-wise. I could keep hoping.

Then the telephone rang. When your nerves are already tingling from electricity-charged air with a feeling of doom over such weather, a ringing phone in a large animal practice is particularly foreboding. I listened with one ear to what my receptionist might be saying to the caller. My heart dropped to my knees when I heard her repeat to the caller, "You have a cow in trouble?"

I loved my job, and actually enjoyed calf deliveries. A calf delivery can be a hard, fatiguing, nasty job, but I loved it when a calf, doomed to die in utero, would bawl lustily after being extracted in chains from his dam. I loved it when a cow in pain and also doomed if the calf wasn't delivered soon, low-ed to her calf and stood up to clean it with long swipes of her raspy tongue. I loved the grin on the happy owner's face that said this year's cattle profits might not be totally down the drain after all. I really liked calf deliveries. But I didn't like them in a cold, driving rain with lightning dancing overhead and thunder breaking my eardrums. I didn't like those callouts at all.

So, with trepidation in my soul, I listened to the phone exchange in the other room. Leslie put the caller on hold, and turned to me where I now stood in the doorway.

"It's Agnes Brewer," she said. "She's got a cow down trying to calve, and needs some help."

I tried, I really did, not to moan out loud. While I liked Mrs. Brewer, with her good herd of black Angus, I wasn't keen on her ranch. It was in river bottom, and many small creek beds forked through it, making the land awkward to cross on fair days. Add to the fact the ranch was located just about directly under where the muttering clouds were hovering—I couldn't help it; I groaned out loud.

"She says she's got a rope on the cow already," Leslie said helpfully, understanding my reluctance to jump in the truck and head out immediately. Leslie had been on a couple of calf deliveries with me, and had been to Agnes Brewer's interesting piece of terrain. On one occasion, we'd had to abandon the truck and carry equipment across a couple of muddy creek beds and through a boot-sucking pasture to reach a down cow. Leslie could see the clouds in the distance as well as I could. She was sympathetic, but relieved, also, that she would not be called to accompany me on the call. She was the only employee at work that day to man the phones and the front desk. I'd have to go this one alone. I sighed.

"Tell Mrs. Brewer that I'm on my way," I said, setting down my coffee cup and going to the changing room to get my "cow clothes" on. Leslie turned back to the phone, and I checked the sky one more time before going to change. The clouds were still there.

Agnes Brewer's cows were well-fed individuals, and used to having people around them, as Agnes was good at hand feeding cubes to them, and well as being a gentle, easy handler. I didn't anticipate a problem handling the cow. It was the weather that worried me. On the drive to the ranch, 25 miles away, I listened to the radio broadcast of the storm approaching, and ask God to smile, just a little, and hold off the water works until the job ahead of us was done.

Agnes met me at the gate, a rain slicker on but not buttoned up. She closed the gate after I had driven through, then ran around to jump into the passenger seat. Agnes was probably 65 years old, in excellent health, and every bit as agile as a woman 20 years younger. This day she looked grim and worried.

"She's down between where the two creeks run together," she said, jabbing her finger in a direction ahead of us. "I couldn't get her up, but I did put a rope on her. She's about ten feet from the edge of a drop-off. Even if she couldn't get up, I was afraid she'd roll off the edge."

Man, I'd been there, seen that happen, and didn't want to again.

"You done good, Agnes," I assured her. "How close can we get?"

"Pretty close, actually", Agnes answered. "The pasture is fairly dry up to a point. I'll tell you when we reach that point."

I drove slowly, not wishing to drop the front end of my pickup into a shallow runoff ditch, unwilling to risk driving over the edge of a winding creek. We

drove what seemed like half way across her land, before
Agnes threw her left hand up and ordered, "Whoa."
I whoa-ed. The storm was very near, and the mid-
morning sky was as black as ink. So far, the rain
had been cold, short spatterings of wetness with
a little wind to drive it deep into the ground. The
ground was not yet water logged. In the twilight-like
darkness ahead of us lay a black lump. The cow. A
rope stretched between her head and a large pecan
tree. A huge lightning bolt flared, followed by a
blast of thunder that tore the sky open, the thunder
coming so soon after the lightning as to seem to occur
simultaneously.

Ahead of us, the cow appeared to leap straight up
and then down again. I jumped in my seat so high
that without my seat belt on, I might have slammed
my head into the ceiling of the cab. I think Agnes
did. We looked at each other. It was her cow, but my
duty. We each had our arms wrapped tightly around
our own shoulders, almost as if not to touch the metal
parts of the pickup. Slowly, I unfurled my arms, and
reached for the door handle. I swallowed, and grabbed
it. Better to die fast. Nothing happened. I jerked the
handle, and threw the door open. The thunder rolled
overhead, but no lightning strikes seemed as near as the
last one. I eased out of the pickup. I could see Agnes
slinking forward also, head ducked as if to prevent a
bolt of lightning from reaching her kerchiefed head. I
realized I was doing the same thing.

The ground was firm and not too muddy. I trotted
as rapidly as I could in my rubber boots to the cow on
the ground. Agnes had had to tie the cow where she

lay, so she wouldn't get too close to the end of the ditch and fall over into it. She had not been able to make the tie-off anywhere else but on the pecan tree, however, and that tree stood within ten feet of the drop off to the creek. Between the time Agnes had tied her off and us getting to her rescue, the cow had managed to move her labor-racked body to the edge of the creek. The rope had prevented her from sliding over the edge, but her rear end, the tiny front feet of an unborn calf peeking from the vulvar lips, hung over the edge of the creek. Oh, great. What do we do now?

A crack of thunder like the sound of shattering glass magnified to the 10th power split the air, and the sky was lit so brilliantly it was like flood lights had been suddenly turned on, blinding us. It lasted at least two full seconds. Fear ran up a banner up my backbone and waved it. This cow had to be saved, now. While the sky still crackled from the effects of the ruptured sound barrier, and the lightning still zagged downward, I reached and grabbed the cow's tail, sat back, and pulled.

Adrenaline is a wonderful thing. Effortless it seemed, to swing that 900-pound body away from the creek and over to relatively dry ground. Effortless it was to roll that cow over onto her other side, so that her feet pointed away from the creek. If she tried to get up now, she wouldn't roll into the creek. Now I could work on saving the calf. I did a quick exam of the cow. There, between the protruding hooves of the calf, a small nose was tucked. Why the cow could not deliver the calf, I did not know.

I sprinted for the truck, expecting any moment to be

struck down by a lightning bolt. I threw open the cargo space of my pickup, grabbed the minimum amount of equipment necessary to do this job—chains and a set of handles—forget the gloves, soap, water. This calf was coming before hell and high water had a chance to reach it. I could see Agnes with the cow. She could see that I was carrying my equipment as I hurried to the patient. She waited for me alongside her cow.

I did a more thorough exam, ducking as thunder rolled across the clouds. Two feet, and a nose. I palpated carefully around the calf, searching for whatever was holding it fast. Ah! Two more calf feet where they shouldn't have been, lodged under the calf's chin. I carefully traced the leg attached to one of the wayward feet. I was worried it might to be a twin, trying to force its way out ahead of its sibling, but the leg proved to belong to the presenting calf. OK; the calf was trying to jump into the world with all four feet at the same time. We could fix that. I carefully eased one rear leg back, changed positions, found the other rear leg, and eased it back into the cow's uterus. Suddenly the cow grunted, strained, and the calf literally flew out of her in a heap on the ground beside me.

Was it alive? Yes! Stunned for a moment, it gave a watery bawl and shook its head. The cow came up sternal, and turned her head so she could see the calf. She sang out a long, relieved moo.

Thunder broke open the sky, as lightning tore across the land. Rain fell, so hard it felt like glass shards. Agnes and I both shrieked in terror and distress. I grabbed the calf by its back legs, and ran, dragging it toward the truck. The cow behind us gave a bellow

at our robbing her of her calf, and lunged to her feet.
The rope held her firmly to the tree. At the truck I
attempted and failed to pick up the slippery 60 pounds
of newborn calf to get it on the tailgate. I looked back
to see where Agnes was. She was at the pecan tree,
frantically sawing with a pocketknife at the rope that
still held her cow, now up and fighting her restraint.
The rope popped in two, the cow staggered backwards
a few feet, then turned, bawled into the pouring rain,
and started trotting toward the truck and her calf.
Agnes ran too, slowing slightly to scoop up the chains
and handles I had not used but had left lying near the
cow. She galloped up beside me, tossing the equipment
into the bed. Together we hefted the wiggling calf up
onto the truck tailgate, rain pelting us, the cow trying
to lick the calf.

Agnes nimbly leapt up and landed bottom first,
feet over the edge, on the tailgate next to the calf. She
grabbed the calf firmly under one arm, and latched the
fingers of her other hand tightly on the side rail of the
truck. "Drive! Drive!" she screamed over the storm.

I raced to the cab, leapt in, cranked the engine,
and floored it. In the rear view mirror I saw Agnes
lurch but hold steady. Behind us, the cow was coming,
and the truck's spinning tires flung mud all over her
face and chest. She never slowed down, but bellowed
indignantly, and followed her truck-riding calf at a trot.
I don't know how we got out of that muddy pasture,
except maybe by the grace of God and a team of his
hardest working angels, but we did. We drove up to
the gate Agnes had latched shut earlier, and I threw the
truck into park, jumped out, ran to the gate, swung it

wide, ran back to the truck, and jumped in again. The cow had barely caught up with us as I gassed the engine again, once again spewing her with mud off the rear tires. She didn't seem to care; as long as her calf was moving away from her, she was going to try to catch up. We took the turn into the barnyard on two wheels. I do not know how Agnes had stayed on board, and did so while clinging to a slimy newborn calf, but she had. She jumped off the tailgate. The cow skidded to a halt next to her calf, singing her cow song, snuffling her offspring, her heavy breath spraying the muddy water that ran off her nose. Agnes ran and opened the barn door, and I dragged the lively calf into the barn. A horse stall would provide shelter for the calf. The cow came as far as the barn door, and stuck her head in, lo-ed at the calf, then followed it into the stall. The cow was so focused on her calf she paid me no mind as I scurried past her and out of the stall. Agnes swung the stall door closed as I scooted out.

For a few minutes we two women stood leaning against the stall wall, heaving in great lung-fuls of air, water cascading from our heads and clothing. Agnes had never taken the time to snap her rain slicker closed, and she was almost as wet as I was. I was totally drenched head to toe, the water having run into my boots as well as soaking me to the skin. We looked at each other, assessed each other, and both of us burst out laughing at the same time. What an adventure!

The cow was licking her calf vigorously, and the calf was protesting in squeaky calf bawls. He struggled to get to his feet. Both Agnes and I were delighted to have rescued both the cow and the calf, but the cold rainwater soaking us was taking its toll. I was starting to shake like a leaf. My fingers were turning blue, and I figured if I looked half as miserable as I felt, I was looking pretty bad. Agnes had drawn her slicker tight around herself, and was vibrating from the chill.

"We have to get the rope off the cow," I said through chattering teeth.

Agnes waved her hand in dismissal. "I'll get it off her later," she said, "when I come back to give her some hay and water. Let's you and me get to the house, get some hot tea."

I eagerly accepted the invitation. I knew she'd give me a towel and a dry shirt. We opened the outer barn door, and looked out into the driving rain toward her house, which looked to be a hundred miles away. About that moment, the rain slacked up considerably. We dashed for the house.

Agnes set the kettle on the stove while I toweled my hair. She had cranked the house's heat system into high before she got us each towels. She was still quite excited about the outcome of the callout, and threw in an apology every once and again. I was so happy to be inside, out of the rain, I almost didn't mind that I was still drenched and cold. The anticipation of a cup of hot tea was already warming me up from the inside. Just as the kettle began to whistle from the water boiling in it, Agnes' phone rang. She set the two cups she had gotten down from the cabinet on the table, and answered the phone.

"Hello?" she said, wiping her hands on a cloth. "Dr. Cooper-Chase? Yes, she's still here. Hold on a minute." Agnes turned toward me. She passed the phone to me.

"It's your office," she said, apparently not picking up on my look of dismay. I took the phone tentatively from her.

It was Leslie. She was very apologetic for calling me, but another client had an animal in trouble. Who, and what? I asked.

"Mrs. Wyatt", she answered. "She's got a cow trying to calve."

I think I went pale. I looked out the window of Agnes' kitchen. The storm was passing by, but it was headed down the road, and probably getting ready to set up camp over Mrs. Margaret Wyatt's ranch, south of where I sat in Agnes Brewer's kitchen.

"Tell her," I said slowly, not really wanting to say it, "tell her I'll be there as soon as possible." I hung up the phone. Agnes looked extremely sympathetic as she held the steaming cup of tea out to me.

"Take it with you," she said. "I'll get the cup next time I come to town."

I nodded numbly, gratefully took the warmth-giving cup, and walked to the door. The rain had stopped coming down over the Agnes Brewer homestead. South of us, in the direction I must now travel, the heavy black clouds boiled and rolled, lightning flashing from their depths. I took a deep breath, stumbled outside to the truck, got in, cranked the motor, slid the heater knob to full blast, put the truck in reverse, waved at Agnes, and pulled out of her yard.

The truck heater did its best, but the rain had been cold and drenching, and I shivered uncontrollably in my wet clothes as I drove. It was 30 miles to Margaret Wyatt's place. She was another of my good female ranchers. Where were the men, I wondered? Why were women out checking their cows in the rain? Were the men safe inside, huddled down with hot drinks, chuckling over the foolhardiness of women ranchers out in such wet weather? I fumed a little over my perceived injustice of it, and picked up the speed a little, racing the clouds to the Wyatt place.

The scenario at Margaret's was pretty much like it had been at Agnes'; the black clouds scudding low, the sky at just past midday looking very much like a late evening sky. But Oh Joy! Margaret's 12-year-old son, Robbie, was at the gate, holding it open for me, so I did not have to dismount from the truck to open it. Margaret's ranch was on higher ground, and I expected it to be a little drier. I drove through the gate and stopped, waiting for Robbie to close the gate and climb in the passenger seat. Robbie was a good boy, helpful to his mother, and a bonafide talker. He was already chatting excitedly as he hopped into the truck.

"Mom's with the cow!" he crowed. "It's old Vanessa. She won't get up. Mom thinks the calf is backwards!" He stopped to draw breath.

"Where is she?" I asked quickly.

"The Bottom!" he answered. "She laid down in the dry creek bed a couple of hours ago, but it started flooding, and Mom couldn't get her to stand up and get out of the water!"

Oh my. I put the pedal to the metal, and the truck lurched forward, bouncing over the rough ground. Robbie was having a good time, hanging on to his seat as the truck rose and fell over the rough ground. He directed me over the field and through another gate, to a pasture that dipped down toward a normally dry creek bed, a creek bed that didn't see water unless the rains had come hard further up stream. I had been "upstream," and had seen the rains come. Overhead, the clouds circled, as if looking for just the right place to drop their payload. On the ground, water was coursing across the pasture, heading for the cow and the woman in the creek.

Vanessa was an old cow, just like Robbie said. I had been thinking she wasn't going to make another year for the past three years now. She had been Margaret's high school show calf, and Margaret had a deep and abiding love and respect for the old Brangus-cross cow. Most of Vanessa's deep red hair had faded to an orangey hue as advancing age replaced much of the red with white hairs. I figured she had to be at least 19 years old. She was far too old to be calving in a wet pasture bottom.

As if reading my thoughts, Robbie spoke up. "Mom had her in the pen for two weeks now," he informed me. "She didn't act like she was ever going to have that calf, so Mom let her out to graze down here for a little while. When she didn't come back this morning, we had to find her. Mom found her lying down in the creek bed. You couldn't even see her at first. We got her to go this far, before she laid down again, and she wouldn't get up. Mom came back to the house to call you."

I could see the cow and her owner ahead of us. We bounced to a halt near to the cow. Upon seeing a strange vehicle in her vicinity, the cow sat up onto her chest, and swung her old, long face toward us. She was a terribly sad looking cow. Margaret jogged over to the truck.

"She broke water about two hours ago," she said, as I climbed out of my truck. Apparently neither she nor Robbie noticed I was still soaking wet, my clothes plastered to me. I was shivering slightly. My hair was still dripping water, in spite of the toweling I'd given it in Agnes' kitchen. Their concern was for their own cow, not that I blamed them.

"I couldn't get her to stand up at first," Margaret continued. "She had a real hard time getting this far, but she fell here, and that's it." She pointed to the north. "Storm's coming, too," she added about the obvious.

The clouds looked like they were coming in for a landing. Water from rains further north were cascading down the creek bed, and the rapidly flowing stream was being broken into two by the bulk of the cow, who lay still on her chest, her thoughts turned inward to the wrongly positioned calf.

"Let's try to get her out of here," I said, and together we urged the cow to rise with slaps and whoops. She gave a half-hearted lunge, and settled back down on the ground. I ran to my truck for my equipment, Robbie pacing me, coming to help carry things I might need. At that moment, as I handed some small things to Robbie, a sharp ping! sounded, then another, and another. Hail had begun pelting us and was pinging off the metal of the truck.

"Robbie! Get in the truck!" I shouted. "Margaret! Come get in the truck! It's hailing!" Robbie was already in the cab, and the hailstones, not bigger than marbles, began to bang down in earnest. I shielded my head, and ducked into the cab with Robbie.

Unbelievably, Margaret was not only staying out in the storm, she was standing up, hunched over, holding her rain coat over Vanessa the cow's head, shielding her for the stinging pellets of ice. The cow never moved, nor did the woman, as the ice shower beat down upon them. In just a few minutes, it passed. I got out of the pickup. The ground was white with ice balls, small and slippery. Robbie slid out from his side of the pickup and trotted toward his mother.

From the north was a roar. We looked in that direction. Margaret lowered her coat and straightened up, turning with her son and me to see what was coming.

Water. A wall of water was coursing down the dry creek bed at about three feet in height. It carried sticks and small logs and rafts of woodland trash made of leaves and pine needles. It washed down the pasture in a brown torrent. Robbie did not need instructions to get in the pickup. He turned and ran and almost dived through the window of the truck into the seat.

"Margaret!" I screamed. "GET UP HERE!"

The water was coming fast. I ran down as close to the cow and the woman as I dared.

"MARGARET!" I called again.

She waved me back, and slogged through the water to the head of her beloved cow. She knelt down, facing the cow, took the cow's chin, raised it high, and set it on her own shoulder. She wrapped her arms firmly around the cow's neck, and clasped her hands together tightly. And she knelt there and waited for the brown flood to hit her and the cow.

I had no idea what to do. I could only wonder, what was she thinking? Could she really believe she could save this old, crippled cow? Did she really want to die like that in front of her young son? The water hit the rear of the cow, splashed and parted around her, washed over her back and slammed into Margaret. The cow disappeared. The woman's head stayed up a moment, and then the pull of the water flipped her backwards, and down she went, still trying to hold onto that cow's neck.

I put my hands over my mouth, afraid to scream, afraid to look back and see Robbie's frightened face, afraid of what I would see as the water slowed and receded and banked away from the higher rolls of the pasture.

Almost as quickly as it hit, the wall of water disappeared, churning down the creek, taking its trash along with it. And surfacing maybe 15 feet further down stream came a reddish cow with a woman clinging desperately to her neck.

I ran as fast as I could toward them. Behind me I heard the truck door open and slam closed, and the running of a young boy's feet. He never uttered a word.

We got to the cow. Margaret was choking and gasping and spitting out dirty brown water. A fine trickle of blood flowed from a minor gash on her forehead. She slowly relinquished her grip on her cow.

And Vanessa mooed, long and low, and shook her long ears to rid them of the water that had entered them. She was on slightly higher ground, and the water was returning to the former level of 12 inches.

Margaret grabbed her son and hugged him fiercely,

and he clung to her wet clothes desperately.

"Did you see what your momma did?" Margaret asked her son, holding his face between her hands, looking him right in the eye. "Did you see that?" He nodded numbly.

"Good," she said. "And I don't EVER want you to do anything even remotely as stupid as that as long as you live." She patted his shoulder fiercely, fondly, then turned to me.

"Can we save the calf?" she asked.

I was still speechless from what I had just seen. I looked at the cow, who regarded me gravely. She grunted and strained. Nothing showed.

"Come on, Robbie", I said. "We have to deliver this calf before this rain starts falling in earnest." We ran for the truck, got the equipment and supplies we needed, and ran back to the cow.

Fortunately, even though it was a breech presentation, the calf was small with lots of room to move around in the cow. As thunder threatened and lightning flashed, I lay behind the cow on the cold, wet ground, working to deliver the calf. Thunder boomed in response to a close-by lightning bolt, and I asked Margaret and Robbie to get to the safety of the truck. I'd have the calf in a minute. Robbie turned and ran for the truck like a scared rabbit, but Margaret lingered. Lightning flared again, and Margaret flattened herself out on the ground next to me. At first, due to the extreme stress I was under, I thought Margaret had been struck by the lightning. When she slid her arms off her head and raised her widened, scared eyes to me, I knew that it wasn't so. She took a chain handle, and indicated she was willing to stay and help deliver the calf. I wasn't going to refuse her help. I got one of the calf's legs in position, and then the other, and in a minute a little heifer calf slide into the world.

No sooner did we have the chains off the calf did the sky open and drop its heavy burden of rain. It felt more like a waterfall than a rainstorm. We dragged/slid the calf toward the truck, and heaved it onto the bed. Behind us, Vanessa bawled for her calf, and struggled gallantly to her feet. She had a little wobble in her rear legs, but without the calf pressing down on nerves in her pelvis, she was able to stand and walk. The muddy ground slowed her just a little as she hurried after her calf.

"Robbie!" I hollered. "Can you drive this truck?"

"Yes Ma'am!" he answered strongly.

"Can he?" I asked Margaret.

She nodded. "He can drive anything," she said.

"Robbie!" I hollered. "Get us out of here!" While he slid excitedly over to the driver's side, I ran and got my equipment, pitched it into the bed of the truck, and hopped up on the tail gate next to Margaret, who sat clutching the calf, bent over, shielding it from the worst of the rain. The cow would follow the truck.

Robbie did a good job of getting the truck back to the front gate without getting us stuck or causing either of us or the calf to bounce off the tailgate. By time we got to the road, the rain had abated somewhat. In short order the cow and calf were safely stashed under a lean-to near the house.

I don't know if Margaret was aware of me at all. She was deeply concerned with her cow and calf, though obviously relieved and happy to have both of them safe. She sent Robbie after towels to dry the calf and hay and water for the cow. I waited a little, delighted to see the newborn calf snorting and shaking the water off its head. I was freezing, though, and backed away to my pickup, climbed aboard it, and drove out of the farmyard, heading for home. What a day.

Margaret stopped by the clinic the following morning, embarrassed for having offered me no hot drink, no towel, and forgetting to pay her bill. I wasn't worried about her. Folks with that much concern for a simple beast such as a cow will almost all come around and take care of their affairs later.

✳

I could always work for people like Margaret Wyatt and Agnes Brewer, and for folks like the Drummonds, the Duvalls, and of course, the old folks like Mr. Martin and Hattie McCloud. There are many other good men and women, too, that I haven't mentioned in these stories. Their care and concern for the animals under their husbandry are what I remember most about the call-outs to assist in veterinary medical crises and routine procedures. The cold and the damp, the heat with its headaches and sweat, the sore muscles and enormous fatigue, the bad roads and long hours take a back seat in my memory banks when I remember the creatures and the people who asked for my help with them. They're the kind of people I miss, and who make me miss my large animal practice.

About the Author

Rosalie Cooper-Chase had always loved animals; all animals, insects included. She grew up in a large family and was the fourth of the ten children. Horses were the creatures of God she loved most, with cats running a close second. As a teenager she spent as much time as she could at a horse farm not far from their home in eastern North Carolina, helping to feed and groom the horses, milking the cows, and cleaning stalls in exchange for a chance to ride one of the many rideable horses.

The family moved to Texas in 1970, and Rosalie found a job managing a horse farm near Rosenberg, Texas. The attending veterinarian for the horse farm was impressed with Rosalie's work ethic and care of her equine charges, and offered her a job as a vet assistant in his practice, the Rose-Rich Veterinary Clinic, a position she loved and worked at for a number of years. During that time she decided to pursue a degree in veterinary medicine, and in 1982 she was accepted into the veterinary medicine curriculum at Texas A&M University. She graduated with a degree in Veterinary Medicine in 1986.

The first job of her career was as an associate with a mixed animal practice in a small town not far from San Antonio, TX. Wanting to own her own practice, she searched for and found one for sale in Crockett, Texas.

She bought the South Pine Animal Hospital in Crockett in 1987.

Over the years in Crockett, Rosalie rescued numerous cats, many dogs, some good horses, and was given a few calves, piglets, and one sheep.

She was the sole practitioner of SPAH until 2010, when she decided it was the right time to sell it. She worked part-time for the new owner for a few years. She is semi-retired today, having moved across state lines to Colorado with her husband, Jack, due to a job relocation for him. She currently keeps busy with maintaining their property in Colorado as well as enjoying the spectacular natural beauty that Colorado offers.

Rosalie Cooper-Chase, DVM with her two dogs,
Ruby (left) and Ossie (right). (Photo: Sherry Glawson)

www.ingramcontent.com/pod-product-compliance
Lightning Source LLC
Chambersburg PA
CBHW031247090426
42742CB00007B/342